RULERS OF INDIA

Babar

RULERS OF INDIA

Babar

STANLEY LANE-POOLE, M.A

GYAN

Published by

Gyan Publishing House
5, Ansari Road
Daryaganj, New Delhi-110002
Phone: 011-47034999, 9811692060
E-mail: books@gyanbooks.com

Distribution Network
gyanbooks.com
India, USA, Canada, UK, Australia, France

ISBN: 978-81-212-8933-7 (PB)
First Published, 1899

2nd Impression 2023

Printed at: Gyan Press, Delhi.

RULERS OF INDIA BABAR

AUTHOR: STANLEY LANE-POOLE

Rulers of India

EDITED BY

SIR WILLIAM WILSON HUNTER, K.C.S.I., C.I.E.

M.A. (OXFORD), LL.D. (CAMBRIDGE)

BÁBAR

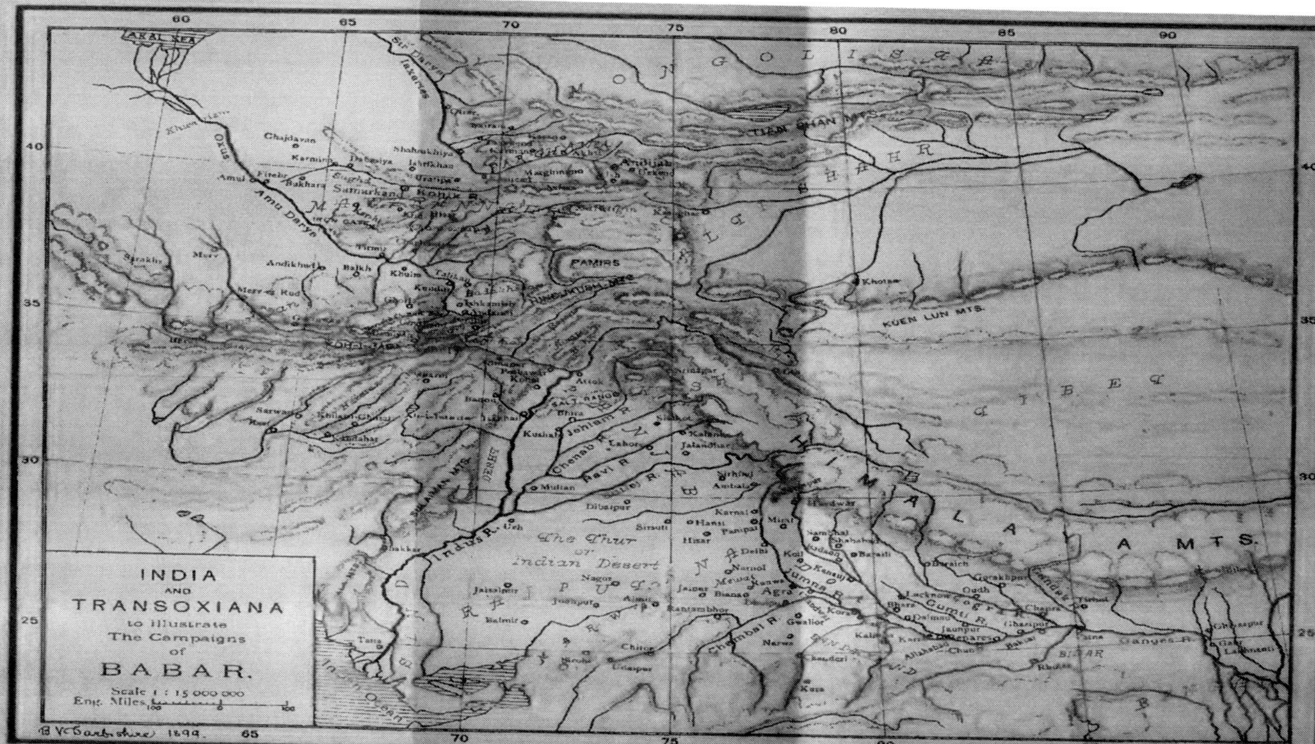
INDIA
AND
TRANSOXIANA
to Illustrate
The Campaigns
of
BABAR.
Scale 1 : 15 000 000
Eng. Miles
ARAL SEA
Oxus
Amu Darya
Sir Darya
Iaxartes
Samarkand
Bukhara
Balkh
Andikhud
Khulm
Kunduz
PAMIRS
HINDUKUSH MTS.
TIEN SHAN MTS.
KUEN LUN MTS.
Khotan
Kashghar
Andijan
Attok
Jehlam R.
Chenab R.
Ravi R.
Lahor
Jalandhar
Multan
Dibalpur
Sirsuti
Hisar
Karnal
Panipat
Delhi
Mirat
Indus R.
The Thur
or
Indian Desert
Agra
Jumna R.
Kanauj
Gwalior
Chambal R.
Chitor
Kalpi
Jaunpur
Benares
Allahabad
Gumti R.
Ghazipur
Patna
Ganges R.
Tatta
Indian Ocean
HIMALAYA MTS.
BIHAR
Barbishire 1899.

BÁBAR

From an Indian drawing of the sixteenth century

RULERS OF INDIA

Bábar

BY

STANLEY LANE-POOLE, M.A.

PROFESSOR OF ARABIC AT TRINITY COLLEGE, DUBLIN

Oxford

AT THE CLARENDON PRESS: 1899

NOTE ON AUTHORITIES

The chief authority for Bábar's life is his own Memoirs or Commentaries, the *Wakái'* or *Túzak-i-Bábari*, on which see pp. 12–15. The English translation by Erskine and Leyden, and Pavet de Courteille's French version, are both cited, but not always *verbatim*. The blanks in the Memoirs are to some extent filled by notices in the *Taríkh-i-Rashídi*, a history of the Mongols in Central Asia, written by Bábar's cousin, Mirzá Haidar, and completed within seventeen years after the Emperor's death: this important work has been admirably translated and edited by Professor E. Denison Ross and the late Consul-General N. Elias (1895). The *Tabakát-i-Bábari* of Shaikh Zain-ad-dín is little more than an inflated paraphrase of the later portions of the Memoirs. Bábar's daughter, Gul-badan, who survived her father, also left some interesting Memoirs, which remain in MS. in the British Museum (Or. 166). The *Shaibáni-náma* of Muhammad Sálih (ed. Vambéry, 1885) gives the rhapsodical view of an enemy, and Mirzá Iskandar's history throws light upon Bábar's relations with Sháh Ismá'íl; on which the coins of the period also bear evidence, as interpreted in the late Professor R. Stuart Poole's *Catalogue of Persian Coins in the British Museum* (1887). Farishta, and Abu-l-Fazl (in the *Akbar-náma*), base their narratives upon the Memoirs, with little addition of much consequence, and there are but few supplementary notices in Badáóni and other writers extracted in Elliot and Dowson's great *History of India as told by its own Historians.* Erskine made excellent use of most of the available materials in the first volume of his *History of India* (1854), a most scholarly and profound work. Mr. H. G. Keene has also treated the subject ably in his *Turks in India* (1879). Essays relating to Bábar have been published by Silvestre de Sacy, Darmesteter (*Journal Asiatique,* 1888, 1890), Teufel (*Z. D. M. G.* xxxvii); and also by Mr. H. Beveridge (*Calcutta Review,* 1897), to whom, through Sir W. W. Hunter, I am indebted for bibliographical information. Unfortunately there was no European traveller who visited Bábar's court either in Farghána, or Kábul, or Agra, and we are thus deprived of the advantage of a western estimate of his person and character.

The map is based upon several sources: my own map of mediaeval India, published in my *Catalogue of Indian Coins in the British Museum*; Mr. Elias's admirable map of Central Asia in the *Taríkh-i-Rashídi*; Sir H. Yule's map in Wood's *Oxus*; Waddington's map prefixed to Erskine's translation of Bábar's Memoirs; and my map of Western Asia (No. 81) in the *Historical Atlas* edited by my brother (Oxford, 1899).

The portrait is from the MS. in the British Museum (Add. 5,717, fol. 52), and though probably not earlier than the end of the sixteenth century, doubtless represents a tradition, and probably copies an earlier miniature. The British Museum possesses a magnificent copy (Or. 3,714) of the best Persian translation of the Memoirs, illustrated by a series of sixty-eight exquisitely beautiful pictures of scenes in Bábar's life, painted chiefly by Hindu artists of the time of Akbar, some of whom are mentioned by Abu-l-Fazl in the *Áín-i-Akbari.*

S. L.-P.

TRINITY COLLEGE, DUBLIN, *May*, 1899.

CONTENTS

THE EMPEROR BÁBAR

CHAPTER I

Introduction

'In the month of Ramazán of the year eight hundred and ninety-nine [June, 1494], I became King of Farghána.' Such are the opening words of the celebrated Memoirs of Bábar, first of the 'Moghul' Emperors of Hindústán.

Bábar is the link between Central Asia and India, between predatory hordes and imperial government, between Tamerlane and Akbar. The blood of the two great Scourges of Asia, Chingiz and Tímúr, mixed in his veins, and to the daring and restlessness of the nomad Tatar he joined the culture and urbanity of the Persian. He brought the energy of the Mongol, the courage and capacity of the Turk, to the listless Hindu; and, himself a soldier of fortune and no architect of empire, he yet laid the first stone of the splendid fabric which his grandson Akbar achieved.

His connexion with India began only in the last

twelve years of his life. His youth was spent in ineffectual struggles to preserve his sovereignty in his native land. His early manhood, passed in his new kingdom of Kábul, was full of an unsatisfied yearning for the recovery of his mother country. It was not till the age of thirty-six that he abandoned his hope of a restored empire on the Oxus and Iaxartes, and turned his eyes resolutely towards the cities and spoils of Hindústán. Five times he invaded the northern plains, and the fifth invasion was a conquest. Five years he dwelt in the India he had now made his own, and in his forty-eighth year he died.

His permanent place in history rests upon his Indian conquests, which opened the way for an imperial line; but his place in biography and in literature is determined rather by his daring adventures and persevering efforts in his earlier days, and by the delightful *Memoirs* in which he related them. Soldier of fortune as he was, Bábar was not the less a man of fine literary taste and fastidious critical perception. In Persian, the language of culture, the Latin of Central Asia, as it is of India, he was an accomplished poet, and in his native Turki he was master of a pure and unaffected style alike in prose and verse[1]. The Turkish princes of his time prided

[1] His cousin, Mirzá Haidar, himself the author of a famous history, wrote of him that he was 'adorned with various virtues and clad with numberless excellences, above all which towered bravery and humanity. In the composition of Turki poetry he was

themselves upon their literary polish, and to turn an elegant *ghazal*, or even to write a beautiful manuscript, was their peculiar ambition, no less worthy or stimulating than to be master of sword or mace. In some of the boldly sketched portraits of his contemporaries which enliven the Memoirs, Bábar often passes abruptly from warlike or administrative qualities to literary gifts; he will tell how many battles a king fought, and then, as if to clinch the tale of his merits, he will add that he was a competent judge of poetry and was fond of reading the *Sháh Náma*, yet had such a fist that 'he never struck a man but he felled him.' Of another dignitary he notes regretfully that 'he never read, and though a townsman he was illiterate and unrefined'; on the other hand 'a brave man' is commended the more because he 'wrote the *nasta'lík* hand,' though, truly, 'after a fashion.' Wit and learning, the art of turning a quatrain on the spot, quoting the Persian classics, writing a good hand, or singing a good song, were highly appreciated in Bábar's world, as much perhaps

second only to Amír 'Ali Shír. He has written a *díván* in the purest and most lucid Turki. He invented a style of verse called *mubaiyan*, and was the author of a most useful treatise on jurisprudence which has been generally adopted. He also wrote an essay on Turki prosody, more elegant than any other, and versified the Rasála-i-Válidiya of his Reverence. Then there is his *Wakái*, or Turki 'Memoirs,' written in a simple, unaffected, yet very pure style. He excelled in music and other arts. Indeed, no one of his family before him ever possessed such talents, nor did any of his race perform such amazing exploits or experience such strange adventures.' (*Tarikh-i-Rashídi*, Ross and Elias.)

as valour, and infinitely more than virtue. Bábar himself will break off in the middle of a tragic story to quote a verse, and he found leisure in the thick of his difficulties and dangers to compose an ode on his misfortunes. His battles as well as his orgies were humanized by a breath of poetry.

Hence his Memoirs are no rough soldier's chronicle of marches and countermarches, 'saps, mines, blinds, gabions, palisadoes, ravelins, half-moons, and such trumpery'; they contain the personal impressions and acute reflections of a cultivated man of the world, well read in Eastern literature, a close and curious observer, quick in perception, a discerning judge of persons, and a devoted lover of nature; one, moreover, who was well able to express his thoughts and observations in clear and vigorous language. 'His autobiography,' says a sound authority [1], 'is one of those priceless records which are for all time, and is fit to rank with the confessions of St. Augustine and Rousseau, and the memoirs of Gibbon and Newton. In Asia it stands almost alone.' There is no doubt a vast deal of dreary chronicle in the Memoirs, much desultory trifling, some repetition, and needlessly minute descriptions of secondary characters and incidents; the first part is infinitely better than the end; but with all this, the shrewd comments and lively impressions which break in upon the narrative give Bábar's reminiscences a unique and penetrating flavour. The man's own

[1] Mr. H. Beveridge, *Calcutta Rev.*, 1897.

character is so fresh and buoyant, so free from convention and cant, so rich in hope, courage, resolve, and at the same time so warm and friendly, so very human, that it conquers one's admiring sympathy. The utter frankness of self-revelation, the unconscious portraiture of all his virtues and follies, his obvious truthfulness and fine sense of honour, give the Memoirs an authority which is equal to their charm. If ever there were a case when the testimony of a single historical document, unsupported by other evidence, should be accepted as sufficient proof, it is the case with Bábar's Memoirs. No reader of this prince of autobiographers can doubt his honesty or his competence as witness and chronicler.

Very little is known about the mode in which they were composed. That they were written at different dates, begun at one time and taken up again after long intervals, as leisure or inclination suggested, is to be inferred from the sudden way in which they break off, generally at a peculiarly critical moment, to be resumed without a word of explanation at a point several years later. The style, moreover, of the later portions is markedly different from that of the earlier, whilst the earlier portions bear internal evidence of revision at a later date. The natural (though conjectural) inference is that the Memoirs were written at various dates; that the earlier part was revised and enlarged after Bábar's invasion of India, though memory failed or time was wanting to fill the gaps; and that the later part remains in its original form of a rough diary because its author died before he had leisure or energy to revise it. The Memoirs were written in Turki, Bábar's native tongue. A copy of the work was in his cousin Haidar's hands, who probably obtained it during his visit to India within ten years of its author's death. Another copy, which appears to be the original of all the existing manuscripts, was transcribed from an original in Bábar's own handwriting by his eldest son, the Emperor Humáyún, in 1553, as is stated in an interpolation by Humáyún in the body of the work[1]. That the son was a faithful copyist is evident, for he has not suppressed several passages in which his own conduct is censured by his father.

The Memoirs were more than once translated from Turki into Persian; notably, with scrupulous accuracy, by the illustrious Mirzá Abdu-r-Rahím, son of Bairam Khán, in 1590, by the desire of the Emperor Akbar. The close agreement, even in trifling details, of the various Turki and Persian manuscripts preserved in several collections, shows that the original text has been faithfully respected, and such variations as exist do not affect the essential accuracy of the document. Even the gaps in the narrative unfortunately occur at the same places and for the same intervals in all the manuscripts, Turki and Persian, with the exception of two or three short but interesting passages which one Turki text alone presents.

[1] *Memoirs*, Erskine and Leyden, 303; Pavet de Courteille, ii. 159.

This text was printed at Kazan by M. Ilminski in 1857, and was translated into French by M. Pavet de Courteille in 1871. Long before this, a translation into vigorous English, by John Leyden and William Erskine, based upon a collation of Persian and Turki manuscripts, and enriched with a valuable introduction and copious notes, appeared in 1826, and has ever since held its place as the standard version[1]. It represents the Persian more than the Turki text, but how little the two differ, and how trifling are the emendations (save in Turki words and names) to be gained from the Turki version, may be seen by a comparison of the French and English translations.

This comparison of two versions founded upon several manuscripts written in two languages brings us to the remarkable conclusion that Bábar's Memoirs have come through the ordeals of translation and transcription practically unchanged. We possess, in effect, the *ipsissima verba* of an autobiography written early in the sixteenth century by one of the most interesting and famous men of all Asia. It is a literary fact of no little importance. The line of Emperors who proceeded from Bábar's loins is no more. The very name of Mongol has lost its influence on the banks of Iaxartes; the Turk is the servant of the Russian he once despised. The last Indian sovereign of Tímúr's race ended his inglorious

[1] It was abridged by Mr. R. M. Caldecott, 1844, in a readable *Life of Bábar.*

career an exile at Rangoon; a few years later, the degenerate descendants of Chingiz Kaán submitted to the officers of the Tsar. The power and pomp of Bábar's dynasty are gone; the record of his life—the *littera scripta* that mocks at time—remains unaltered and imperishable.

CHAPTER II

Farghána

1494

In 1494 Bábar inherited the kingdom of Farghána from his father, 'Omar Shaikh, a son of Abú-Sa'íd, the great-grandson of the Amír Tímúr or Tamerlane.

A hundred years had passed since the Barlás Turk, in a series of triumphant campaigns, had made himself master of the western half of Asia, from Káshghar on the edge of the terrible mid-Asian desert, to the cliffs of the Aegean sea. He had driven the Knights of Rhodes out of their castle at Smyrna, and had even marched into India and sacked Delhi. In 1405 he was on his way to subdue China and set all the continent of Asia beneath his feet, when death intervened. Tímúr's conquests were too recent, too hasty and imperfect, to permit the organization of a settled empire. They were like a vast conflagration driven before the wind, which destroys the herbage for a while; but when the flame has passed away, the earth grows green again. Many of the princes, who had fled before the blast of Tímúr's hurricane, came back to their old seats when the destroyer was departed; and it was only over part of Persia and over the country beyond the Oxus that his descendants maintained their hold when that iron hand was stiff. Even there, a single century witnessed their universal downfall; the fire had only left some embers, which smouldered awhile, but, lacking the kindling and stirring of the great incendiary, finally died out. After that, the sole relic of Tímúr's vast dominion was the little kingdom which an exiled prince of his own brave blood set up among the crags and passes of the Afghán hills, whence came the 'Great Moghuls' and the glories of Delhi and Agra.

Bábar in exile founded a grandiose empire, but Bábar in the home of his forefathers was but a little prince among many rivals. Every one of the numerous progeny of Tímúr was a claimant to some throne. Mawaránnaḥr or Transoxiana—the land of the two great rivers, Oxus and Iaxartes, the Amu and Sir Darya of to-day—was a cockpit for the jealousy and strife of a multitude of petty princes, who, whether they called themselves Mirzás in Persian, or Kháns in Turki, or plain Amírs in Arabic, resembled one another closely in character and ambition. The character was 'earthly, sensual, devilish'; the ambition was to grasp power and wealth, *quocunque modo rem*, at the sacrifice of kindred, faith, and honour.

Over this crew of scheming adventurers, the King of Samarkand endeavoured to maintain some show of authority. This was Sultán Ahmad Mirzá[1], Bábar's

[1] Sultán was a common title among Turkish and Persian princes and nobles, and did not imply the supreme sovereignty of an

uncle, a weak easy-going toper, managed by his Begs or nobles. He represented the central power of Tímúr's empire, but he represented a shadow. Further east, from his citadel of Hisár, Ahmad's brother Mahmúd ruled the country of the Upper Oxus, Kunduz, and Badakhshán, up to the icy barrier of the Hindú Kúsh. A third brother, Ulugh Beg, held Kábul and Ghazní; and a fourth, Bábar's father, 'Omar Shaikh, was King of Farghána, or as it was afterwards called Khókand. His capital was Andiján, but he was staying at the second city, Akhsi, when happening to visit his pigeons in their house overhanging the cliff, on June 9, 1494, by a singular accident the whole building slid down the precipice, and he fell ingloriously to the bottom 'with his pigeons and dovecote, and winged his flight to the other world.' Besides these four brothers, Sultán Husain Baikará, a cousin four times removed, ruled at Herát, with much state and magnificence, what was left of the Tímúrid empire in Khurásán, from Balkh near the Oxus to Astarábád beside the Caspian sea.

These were the leading princes of Tímúr's race at the time of Bábar's accession; but they do not exhaust the chief sources of political disturbance. Further east and north the Mongol tribes, still led by descendants of Chingiz Kaán, mustered in multitudes in their

Osmánli Sultán. Mirzá *after* a name connotes royal blood. In general the full style, such as Sultán Mahmúd Mirzá, &c., will here be curtailed to the essential name Mahmúd, &c., or Mahmúd Mirzá when a distinction is needed from Mahmúd Khán.

favourite grazing steppes. Yúnus Khán, their chief, who owed his position to Bábar's paternal grandfather, had given three of his daughters in marriage to three of the brothers we have named, and one of them was the mother of Bábar. The connexion in no degree hampered the Mongols' natural love of war, and Mahmúd Khán [1], who had succeeded his father Yúnus on the white pelt or coronation seat of the tribes, played a conspicuous part in the contests which distracted Bábar's youth. Yet Mahmúd Khán, for a Mongol, was a man of sedate and civilized habits, who abhorred the rough life of the tents, and held his court in the populous city of Táshkend, a little north of his nephew's dominions. His defection sorely galled the Mongol patriots, but fortunately his younger brother Ahmad Khán had his full share of the national passion for the wastes, and to him was drawn the fealty of the clans who retained their primitive customs in the plains to the east of Farghána. He, too, mixed in the struggles of the time, and like his brother Mahmúd fixed his eyes on Samarkand, the stately capital of Tímúr, whilst both felt the Mongol's fierce delight in mere fighting.

Besides these chiefs who were entitled, by descent from Chingiz or Tímúr, to wrangle over their inheritance, there were many minor nobles who had no such

[1] The Turkish title Khán distinguishes these Mongol chiefs from their Persianated relations in Transoxiana. Thus Mahmúd *Khán* was Bábar's maternal uncle, of Táshkend; Mahmúd *Mirzá* was Bábar's paternal uncle, of Hisár.

title, but, like the Dughlát Amírs of Káshghar and Uratipa—Mongols of blue blood—or the Tarkháns of Samarkand, came of a privileged family, and, if not the rose, were so near it that they often plucked its petals. And beyond these, like a cloud on the horizon, gathered the Uzbeg tribes of Turkistán and Otrár, on the lower Iaxartes,—soon to overshadow the heritage of Tímúr, and under their great leader, Shaibáni Khán, to become the most formidable power on the Oxus,—the one power before which even Bábar turned and fled.

In the midst of the confusion and strife of so many jarring interests, the child of eleven suddenly found himself called upon to play the part of king. Of his earlier years hardly anything is known. He was born on the 6th of Muharram, 888, St. Valentine's day, 1483[1]. A courier was at once sent to bear the good news to his mother's father, Yúnus, the Khán of the Mongols, and the grand old chief of seventy years came to Farghána and joined heartily in the rejoicings and feasts with which they celebrated the

[1] 'Omar Shaikh had three sons and five daughters by five of his wives and concubines:

'OMAR SHAIKH =

= Kutluk Nigár Khánum (Mongol, dau. of Yúnus Khán), d. 1505: *Khanzáda Begum*, b. 1478; Zahír-ad-dín Muhammad BÁBAR, b. Feb. 14, 1483.

= Fátima Sultán (Mongol): Jahángir Mirzá, b. 1485.

= Umaid Aghácha (concubine, of Andiján): *Mihrbánu Begum*, b. 1478; Násir Mirzá, b. 1487; *Shehrbánu Begum*, b. 1491.

= Aghá Sultán (concubine): *Yádgár Sultán Begum*, b. posth. 1494.

= Sultán Makhdúm Karaguz (concubine): *Rukhiya Sultán Begum*, b. posth. 1494.

shaving of his grandson's head. As the ill-educated Mongols could not pronounce his Arabic name—Zahír-ad-dín Muhammad—they dubbed him 'Bábar.' At the age of five, the child was taken on a visit to Samarkand, where he was betrothed to his cousin 'Áïsha, the infant daughter of Sultan Ahmad; and during this visit, on the occasion of a great wedding, Bábar was sent to pluck the veil from the bride, for good luck. The next six years must have been spent in education, and well spent, for he had little leisure in after years to improve himself, and his remarkable attainments in the two languages he wrote imply steady application. Of this early training we hear nothing, but it is reasonable to suppose that an important part of it was due to the women of his family. The Mongol women retained the virtues of the desert, unspoiled by luxury or by Muhammadanism. They were brave, devoted, and simple; and among the constant references in Bábar's Memoirs to the almost universal habit of drunkenness among the men, we find but one solitary allusion—evidently a reproach—to a woman 'who drank wine.' The women of Bábar's Mongol blood clung to him through all his troubles with devoted fortitude, though his Turkish wives deserted him; and their sympathy in later life must have been the result of tender association in childhood.

Above them all, his grandmother, Isán-daulat Begum, the widow of Yúnus, stood pre-eminent. 'Few equalled her in sense and sagacity,' her grandson says; 'she was wonderfully far-sighted and judicious; many important matters and enterprises were undertaken at her instance.' The story told of her when her husband fell into the hands of his enemy reveals a Spartan character. The conqueror had allotted her to one of his officers, though Yúnus was living. The Begum, however, offered no objection, but received her new bridegroom affably. The moment he was in her room, she had the doors locked, and made her women servants stab him to death, and throw his body into the street. To the messenger who came from the conqueror to learn the meaning of this, she said: 'I am the wife of Yúnus Khán. Shaikh Jamál gave me to another man, contrary to law; so I slew him; and the Shaikh may slay me too if he pleases.' Struck by her constancy, Jamál restored her in all honour to her husband, whose prison she shared for a year, till both were freed.

This great lady was a rock of strength to her grandson in the years of his premature kingship. He was at the Pavilion of the Four Gardens at Andiján when the news of his father's sudden death reached him, in June, 1494. His first thought was to make himself sure of the capital before a brother, an uncle, or some disloyal Beg should take the chance and seize it. He instantly mounted his horse, called a handful of his followers, and rode to the citadel—the vital point to secure. As he drew near, one of his officers caught his rein, and bade him beware of falling into a trap. How could he tell whether the garrison were loyal? He was turning aside to the terrace, to await overtures, when the Begs who held the citadel sent a message of welcome by one of those Khwájas or holy men whose word was as sacred as their influence was profound in the politics of the day. Bábar entered the citadel as king, and they all set to work without delay to put the fortress into a state of defence.

It was not a moment too soon. The little kingdom was menaced on three sides by invasions bequeathed by his hasty-tempered father. Two uncles were already on the march to seize the throne: they had agreed that their quarrelsome brother, 'Omar Shaikh, had become unbearable, and though he had meanwhile made his singular exit from life through the dovecote, they did not change their plans. Ahmad Mirzá advanced from Samarkand; his brother-in-law Mahmúd Khán from Táshkend. Uratipa, Khojend, and Marghinán, in rapid succession opened their gates to Ahmad, and he was close to Andiján at the very time when Bábar got into the castle. Resistance seemed hopeless, and the boy sent an embassy of submission, protesting that he was his invader's 'servant and son,' and begging to be allowed the rank of viceroy over the land where by right he was king. The overture was harshly repelled, and the advance continued. Fortunately for Bábar, a river lay between, a black and turbid stream with a slimy bottom. On the narrow bridge the enemy pressed too eagerly, and many fell over and were drowned. The croakers recalled a disaster that had happened once before to an army on that very bridge in just the same way. Panic seized the superstitious troopers, and they could not be induced to move forward. The horses, too, were done up, and sickness broke out in the camp. Ahmad was no man to face an emergency. He made terms with Bábar, retaining the cities he had taken, and ingloriously made his way homewards, only to die on the road.

Mahmúd Khán, meanwhile, had annexed the northern town of Kásán and was laying siege to Akhsi, the second city of the kingdom. Here he met with an unexpected resistance: the fort was stoutly defended by the Begs of Bábar's father, and Mahmúd, after several assaults, retired to his own country. He was more celebrated for beginning than for achieving a campaign. A third invader, the Dughlát Amír of Káshghar and Khotan, seized Uzkend, and built a fortress to secure it; but Bábar's men had little trouble in dislodging him.

The danger was over, but not the loss. Bábar was now indeed king of Farghána, but his kingdom was shrunk to the eighty miles of rivage between Andiján and Akhsi. The rest had to be won back from his powerful neighbours. For many years he never lost sight of this object. His dearest ambition was, not only to recover his father's realm, but to seat himself at Samarkand on the throne of his great ancestor Tímúr. This was the *grande idée* to which he devoted his youth and early manhood.

To those who imagine the country beyond the Oxus

to be a desert dotted with ruins buried in sand, it may seem an idle dream. They forget that the great provinces, known to the Greeks and Romans as Sogdiana, Margiana, and Bactriana, were a favoured part of Alexander's empire, where more than one Alexandria marked the conqueror's path. Samarkand, Bukhárá, and Balkh were famous cities of antiquity, and throughout the middle ages they were renowned for wealth and commerce, and not less for learning and the arts. The Persian Sámánids had held their splendid court there; Tímúr had enriched Samarkand with the spoils of his universal conquests; he had brought skilled craftsmen and artists from the uttermost parts of Asia to build him 'stately pleasure domes' and splendid mosques; and his capital became one of the most beautiful as it had long been one of the most cultivated cities of the East. Science had found a home in the Oxus province since Fárábi the philosopher and Farghání the astronomer pursued their researches there in the ninth century; and Tímúr's grandson, Ulugh Beg, carried on the tradition by building the observatory at Samarkand where his famous star tables were drawn up for the perpetual information of astronomers. The incomparable Avicenna himself was a Bukhárioté.

Centres of learning are usually centres of plenty. Men of science do not burrow like conies in the desert rocks: they live where the toils of learning may be alleviated by the comforts that attend wealth. The country about the two great rivers and their tributary streams was one of the most fertile in Asia. Farghána itself was prodigal of fruit and laden with heavy harvests. Abundantly watered by the Sir, and sheltered on all sides from the outer world by fostering hills—save where a gap to the south-west opened out towards Samarkand—the little province, smaller than Ireland, was a garden, an orchard, a vineyard. Grapes and melons ripened to perfection at Andiján, innumerable mills plashed in the watercourses and ground the grain yielded by the generous earth. The beautiful gardens of Ush, a day's march to the south, were gay with violets, tulips, and roses in their seasons, and between the brooks the cattle browsed on the rich clover meadows. At Marghinán, a little to the west, the third city of Farghána, grew such apricots and pomegranates that a man would journey from afar to taste them: many years after he was banished from his land, Bábar recalled with a sigh the flavour of the dried apricots stuffed with almonds which were so good at Marghinán. The luscious pomegranates of Khojend were not to be despised, but the melons of Akhsi—who could resist the melons of Akhsi, which had not their equal in the world, not even in the spreading melon fields of Bukhárá? If he thought of the apricots of Marghinán in the days of his exile, Bábar suffered the dreams of a Tantalus when he remembered the lost joys of the melons of Akhsi. But there was more sustaining food than melon-pulp among the hills and woods of his native land. The pastures nourished herds of cattle, sheep and goats cut their devious tracks on the mountain sides, pheasants, white deer, hares, wild goats, gave sport to the hunter and his hawk. Farghána indeed was a land of milk and honey, an oasis of plenty between the deserts of Khiva and the Takla Makán. The snow-capped hills that clipped it tempered its climate, and during the heats of summer welcomed its inhabitants to their cool retreats.

The people with whom the child-king was to dwell were of mixed race and varied character. The old Persian sons of the soil still formed the mass of the population, and tilled the earth for their masters; but they were of so little political account that they were known as 'strangers,' *tájiks,* much as the Saxons miscalled the ancient Britons 'Welsh.' The Tájiks were the hewers of wood and drawers of water for their Mongol and Turkish conquerors. In the towns the same Persian race, under the name of *Sarts*, formed the trading class, and performed the part of general utility. The ruling race was a mixture of those tribes which from time immemorial have migrated from the central steppes and swept over the lands which other folk had made ready for them. They comprised people of the Turkish nations, Uighurs, Naimans, Karluks, with Mongols proper and Kálmaks. When a Khán conquered another Khán he usually took his daughter or widow to wife, and the result of this constant crossing was the gradual obliteration of the distinctive characteristics of race among the upper classes. Yúnus Khán, for example, a Mongol by paternal descent, who ought to have been smooth-cheeked with Mongolian features, was described as having 'a full beard and a Tájik face,' and doubtless he was one of many similar cross-breeds.

Bábar himself was through his mother a grandson of Yúnus, and a descendant of the great Mongol Chingiz Kaán, but on his father's side he came down from Tímúr, the Barlás Turk. The Mongols called him and his kindred 'Chaghatais,' but he always called himself a Turk, and spoke of the Mongols with superb contempt. The Indian empire of the 'Great Moghuls' had not then restored honour to the name, and the Mongols of the pastoral steppes east and north of Farghána must certainly have appeared an uncouth race to the comparatively polished gentlemen of the towns, who wrote charming Persian odes, and had a horror of the discomforts of the deserts. These town 'Turks' (as we must call them, despite their mixed breed) occupied themselves with the pleasures and profits of a governing class. They were intelligent, often cultivated, brave, and energetic; they were also cruel, vicious, and treacherous. As liars they had few equals. They could rarely be trusted if anything was to be gained by betrayal.

The Memoirs contain some spirited portraits of the men among whom Bábar spent his early years. We can see his father, 'Omar Shaikh, almost as clearly as if we had met him: a short 'podgy' monarch, with stubbly brown beard, carelessly dressed, and apt to burst his coat strings in moments of energy or repletion; an assiduous toper, taking kindly to malt liquor, and poppy juice and bhang, but hardly steady in nerve after his two regular drinking bouts a week. A strong man, nevertheless, who never struck out but he floored his man; something of a poet, too, who could turn out a fair copy of verses, and delighted in reading the *Sháh Náma*; in character honest to a fault, but hasty in temper and policy, and too ready to 'change peace for war, and friendship for hatred.' 'His generosity was large,' says his son, 'and so was his whole soul: he was of a rare humour, genial, eloquent, and sweet in his discourse, yet brave withal and manly.' His weakness, besides the bottle, was backgammon.

His court held men of many turns. There was Bábar's tutor, Shaikh Mazíd, 'a great disciplinarian' over others, but himself unbridled in sensual abominations. Khwája Husain was a good-tempered easy-going fellow, of simple habits, who sang a capital song when the wine was going round. He had a genial comrade in Hasan Ya'kúb Beg, who could reel off an ode, was inimitable at leap-frog, played a good game at polo, and was altogether a frank, good-humoured, clever, handy man. They were not all thus, for 'Ali Majíd is described bluntly as 'a vicious, treacherous, good-for-nothing hypocrite'; and the Grand Huntsman, who pretended to sorcery, was a disagreeable, sour-faced, conceited boor, whose vulgarity and insincerity were matched by his meanness and greed of gold. The Great Seal made a pleasing contrast, 'a most witty and humoursome personage—but reckless in debauch.' Kambar[1] 'Ali, once a skinner by trade, seemed to have his wits but skin-deep: 'he talked a great deal, and very idly—a great talker can't help saying foolish things at times—his talents were narrow, and he had a muddy brain.' In spite of this unfortunate peculiarity, Kambar 'Ali served his uncomplimentary master well at many a pinch.

One of Bábar's best sketches is of his uncle Ahmad, the King of Samarkand, who so nearly swallowed up his nephew's inheritance. He was a true Turk, 'tall, ruddy, and corpulent,' bearded only on the chin, and particular about the lie of his turban, which he always wore in the four-plait fashion with the hitch over the eyebrow. He was scrupulously devout, never omitting the regulation-prayers, even between the decanters, and his veneration for his Khwája or spiritual director was such that he would not think of uncrossing his leg, were it never so cramped, whilst they were engaged in serious discourse. Only once did he break this rule, and then it was found that the king had been sitting by chance upon a bone—some relic of a royal banquet—in sore discomfort. He was not intellectual, one must admit, and did not read at all; for a town-bred Turk he was conspicuously illiterate and unrefined; genius had not been lavish to him: but he had the virtues of his defects, he was a plain honest Turk, a man of few words, just and true in his

[1] Written Kanbar, but pronounced Kambar; so Tanbal, Tambal, further on.

dealings, faithful to his treaty, and never swerving by a line from his covenant.

> His words were bonds, his oaths were oracles,
> His heart as far from fraud as heaven from earth.

He was a sportsman, moreover, of rare skill, such as had not been known since Ulugh Beg forgot the intricacies of astronomy in the excitement of the chase. Hawking was his favourite sport, and seldom did his goshawk miss the quarry. He was a famous archer, and a sure marksman when taking a galloping shot at the Mongolian popinjay—a platter set upon a pole. So modest and discreet were his manners that he was never known to let his bare foot peep out from beneath his robes, even in private: yet 'he would drink day and night without a break for twenty or thirty days on end,' not indeed in morose solitude, but in full court, toping jovially among his Begs. Then for an equal interval he would abstain, and comfort his stomach with pungent delicacies, to restore its tone. Unfortunately he had no will of his own, and his boonfellows, who were also his ministers, led him as they pleased, so that he found himself plunged into adventures to which his sober judgement—when it was so—would not have committed him. But Ahmad Mirzá's drinking days were nearly over at the date when this history begins. He died on his way home from his invasion of Bábar's country, and in the struggles that ensued the young prince soon began to play a conspicuous part.

CHAPTER III

Samarkand Won and Lost

1494–1500

In reading the story of Bábar's adventures, two reflections at once arise: in no country or period of history was the influence more obvious of the sentiment or 'divinity' that 'doth hedge a king,' and seldom has a king's personal character responded more generously to the homage. The long obedience of the patient East set a halo of reverence around the youthful sovereign, without which even his indomitable spirit could scarcely have asserted itself; but this obedience of the dumb animal, this time-honoured respect for inherited authority, was transformed among the masses into something like enthusiastic devotion by the brave and noble qualities of the boyish hero. Bábar possessed a power of winning hearts, which stood him in good stead with the many, even when his influence waned among the chiefs.

It seems absurd to treat a child of twelve as if he were a ruler of men, and it would be idle to deny a share in the result to his more mature advisers. But we have seen the characters of some of the men who formed his father's court and afterwards constituted the 'ministry' of the youthful heir, and it is not reasonable to suppose that such men, of their own initiative, could have planned what was demonstrably achieved in Bábar's 'teens.' Most of them, as will appear, were corrupt and self-seeking, and the higher their rank and talents the less trustworthy they became. A sufficient bribe, an opening for power or plunder, or the mere prudence that might save their skin, promoted 'hedging,' and led them to desert their master in critical emergencies.

Ministers and commanders changed, hesitated, intrigued, forsook him, but Bábar remained steadfast. He used their service as long as they yielded it, but if they chose to desert him he had the gift to supply their place. When almost all abandoned him, and none believed in his star, Bábar never lost faith. His serene constancy of purpose, his noble fortitude, are the only invariable elements in the vicissitudes of his early life, the one unfailing antidote to the poison of intrigue. Making every allowance for the temporary and often time-serving assistance of his shifty Begs, we must admit that, despite his absurd youthfulness, the prime cause of his early successes was Bábar himself. After all, a boy in the East has often shown signs of precocious ability. Akbar was not fourteen when he came to the throne; Sulaiman the Great was intrusted with high commands in his youth; and Bábar was but another example of rapid development.

How little even the best among his officers could be trusted was shown when he had hardly mounted the throne. The pleasant-spoken adept at leap-frog, the delight of the polo-field, Hasan Ya'kúb, who had been made prime minister, almost regent, of the realm, began an intrigue to crown Bábar's younger brother Jahángír, as a readier tool to his own ambition,—or to that of his fellow-conspirator, the new King of Samarkand. He forgot that he had to reckon with a shrewd old woman. Bábar's grandmother scented the plot, and the agile minister had to take to his heels; on his way to Samarkand he fell in a skirmish, 'a sacrifice to his own misdeeds,' shot by a chance arrow by his own men. The episode evidently made an impression on the little king, who seems to have taken his responsibilities seriously, and set himself to live by rule: 'This year,' he says, 'I began to abstain from forbidden and doubtful meats, and extended my precautions to the knife, the spoon, and the table-cloth. I also seldom omitted my midnight prayers.'

It was a time when a man might well set his house in order. A period of anarchy, worse even than the disorders of the late reign, was at hand. Ahmad Mirzá had been followed at Samarkand by his brother Mahmúd, and the change was immediately felt. The new king was a cruel tyrant, the murderer of his own kin, an unbeliever, and a shameless debauchee. Ahmad's jovial indiscretions were forgotten in face of the frantic orgies of the new court, where buffoons played obscene pranks in the public gaze, and acted in mimicry the disgusting scenes which were too literally enacted in private. The whole city became corrupt; no child was safe; the army was a hotbed of profligacy, and decency was openly defied. Fortunately the new king died in six months; but if morals were relieved, anarchy still rioted in the struggles of his sons and kindred for the throne. Every one sought to grasp whatever he could reach. In 1495 Samarkand was threatened by four separate invasions. Sultán Husain of Herát crossed over from Persia; one son of Mahmúd advanced in force from Hisár; another hurried up from Bukhárá; and Bábar, not to be left out of the race, recovered Asfará and Khojend, and set his face towards the capital. Nothing came of it that year, beyond an agreement which recalls the treaty of Tilsit. Bábar and his cousin, Sultán 'Ali, distrustful of each other, and guarding against surprise, met on horseback in the middle of the river Kohik, and swore to join hands in an attack on Samarkand in the following year.

Accordingly, in May, 1497, Bábar marched on Samarkand; his ally did not appear, but this did not discourage him. He pitched his camp near the city, and soon found that the tájik inhabitants were not indisposed to welcome him. 'A number of traders and others came from the town, and began buying and selling. One day, about afternoon prayers, there was suddenly a general hubbub, and the whole of these Muslims were plundered. Yet such was the discipline of my army that, on my issuing an order that no one should presume to detain any of the things that had been seized, but that the whole should be restored without reserve before the end of the first watch next day, there was not a piece of thread or a broken needle that was not restored to its owner.' Thenceforward Bábar had the people on his side. They flocked to his camp, till it rivalled in population the capital itself. But Mahmúd's son Baisanghar made a sturdy defence, and many hot skirmishes took place in the shady *Khiyábán* beneath the walls. Shaibáni Khán was induced to bring his Uzbegs from Turkistán to relieve the city; but when Bábar formed up to receive the attack, the Uzbegs thought better of the adventure and went home. At last Baisanghar, 'followed by two or three hundred hungry, naked wretches,' fled from the besieged city, and Bábar entered Samarkand in triumph. This was at the end of November, 1497, when Vasco da Gama was finding his way towards Calicut.

The young conqueror rode to the 'Garden Palace,' where the three estates, the nobles, the divines, and the people, paid him homage. He had his heart's desire; he sat in the throne of Tímúr, in the seat of Alexander 'of the two Horns.' Samarkand, the dream of his life, was his. He must 'mark well her bulwarks,' take stock of her treasures; he paced the spreading ramparts himself, and found them 10,600 paces in circuit; he wandered from palace to palace, from pleasaunce to pleasaunce. The whole land, as far as Bukhárá, seemed one great garden, full of fruits and crops, and teeming with busy workers. The Kohik watered the north side of the city, that fertilizing stream which is now well named Zar-afshán, 'gold-diffusing'; on the south ran the Darghám; frequent canals joined the two. In the demesnes watered by these many streams the Kings of Samarkand had built pleasure-houses, and often they would camp in the fine weather on some soft rich meadow, which they screened from public gaze, and converted for the time into a royal pleasaunce. East of the city were 'Perfect Garden' and 'Heart's Delight'—the Trianon of Tamerlane, adorned with paintings of his Indian wars. In the citadel stood the 'Blue Palace,' where every sovereign was enthroned, and where deposed kings were sent to their doom; so that 'to visit the Guksarái' became an ominous metaphor.

Tímúr's mosque stood hard by the Iron Gate; skilled masons and sculptors from Hindústán and Persia and Asia Minor had set their hands to the building, and the colossal inscription from the Korán over the gate testified to the orthodoxy of the 'Scourge of God.' Near the stone fort is a college, and here lie the bones of Tímúr and his descendants, the Kings of Samarkand. Ulugh Beg's observatory, three stories high, full of the astronomical instruments of the age, overlooked the city from the Hill of Kohik, and in the 'Garden of the Alameida,' at the foot of this hill, rose the tower of the Forty Pillars, *Chihil Sitún*, with its hall and open galleries, raised on twisted and fluted columns. In another garden the 'China House' was lined with tiles from Cathay, and the

'Echo Mosque' perpetually stirred the wonder of the holiday folk, who could not fathom its mysterious reverberations. The gardens of Samarkand, with their wealth of melons, apples, pomegranates, and above all the *Sáhibi* grapes, were famed far and wide; and the industries of its populace were exported to all lands. Each trade had its own bazar, and the best paper in the world and the finest crimson stuffs were to be found in its warehouses.

For just a hundred days Bábar revelled in the delights of his beautiful city, and then he lost it. His troops had counted on a handsome booty, but they found a starving town. 'Samarkand,' he wrote, 'had been taken after a hard and trying siege of seven months. On its capture, indeed, the soldiers took plenty of spoil; but the rest of the country had joined me or Sultán 'Ali of its own accord, and of course had not been given over to plunder. . . Samarkand was in so distressed a state when we took it that we had to supply the inhabitants with seed-corn and food to help them to carry on till the harvest. How could one levy taxes from so exhausted a land? My troops were thus brought to much distress, and I had nothing to give them. They began to think of home; they deserted one by one. . . All the Mongols deserted; and at last Ahmad Tambal himself [a leading Beg, who had been highly honoured and rewarded] took himself off and left me.' Bábar found himself almost alone, with but a thousand followers; to add to his misfortunes he fell ill. For four days he was speechless, and took no nourishment; only his attendants moistened his tongue with a piece of wet cotton.

Meanwhile Tambal and the other deserters had openly revolted and set up Prince Jahángír on the throne of Farghána. Letter after letter was brought to Samarkand entreating Bábar to come to the rescue of Andiján, where his mother and grandmother were closely besieged by the rebels. At last he was sufficiently recovered to set out; but he had barely reached Khojend when he heard that the governor of Andiján, believing his sovereign dead, had surrendered the city. A messenger, who had been incautiously admitted to Bábar's room at Samarkand during his illness, had found him speechless, and returning to Andiján, had naturally reported him to be in the very article of death. Deprived, as they thought, of their king, the garrison made terms with the enemy. They had even signalized their pact by hanging Bábar's envoy, the holy Khwája Kázi, over the gate of the citadel. It was an act of sacrilege, the martyrdom of a saint:

> 'I have no doubt,' says Bábar, 'that Khwája Kázi was a saint. What better proof could be had than the single fact that in a short time of all who were concerned in his murder not a trace or vestige remained? They were absolutely extirpated. He was a wonderfully brave man—which is no mean proof of saintship. Other men, brave as they may be, have some little nervousness or trepidation in them: the Khwája had not a particle of either.'

Nor was this the worst; as soon as Bábar had left

Samarkand, Sultán 'Ali occupied it. His kingdom had vanished at both ends. 'For the sake of Andiján I had lost Samarkand, and I found I had lost the one without saving the other.'

He made many attempts to recover both, but at first utterly in vain. He induced his uncle, Mahmúd Khán (who had an eye on Farghána for himself), to march at the head of his Mongols to his support. The Khán, a poor soldier and worse general, but ever ready to do something, however futile, arrived before Akhsi, where he came to an understanding with the rebels, and turned back again. It was Bábar's last hope, and now he saw his own small army melting away. 'The Begs, captains, and troopers, many of them, had wives and children at Andiján; they saw no chance of our regaining it; and great and small, gentle and simple, to the number of seven or eight hundred men, left me altogether. . . Only two hundred or so of all ranks, good and bad, stuck to me, choosing voluntarily a life of exile and hardship.' After the brief triumph at Samarkand the contrast was too bitter even for his buoyant nature: 'I became a prey to melancholy and vexation,' he writes; 'I was now reduced to a sore distressed state, and wept much.'

He was now no king at all. His only possession was the little town of Khojend; all the rest was in the hands of his enemies. Happily they had spared his family, and his mother and his brave old grandmother now rejoined him. It was not in him to give way to despair: 'Filled as I was by the ambition of conquest and broad sway, one or two reverses could not make me sit down and do nothing.'

> What though the field be lost,
> All is not lost—the unconquerable will,
> And courage never to submit or yield.

He went to Táshkend and borrowed Mongol troops from the Khán, with which he surprised and captured Nasúkh, some forty miles from his little capital. In his worst troubles he was never so sad that he found no comfort in the gifts of nature, and with one of those naïve touches which make his Memoirs so real, he notes that when he took Nasúkh 'it was the season when the melons were ripe,' those delicious Ismá'íl Shaikhi melons, with a 'yellow skin, mottled like shagreen'—'a wonderful delicate and toothsome melon,' he adds. His force was too small to hold his conquest, and he was obliged regretfully to abandon it, but still the success cheered him, and he returned to Khojend in better heart. It soon became clear, however, that he could not go on living there. The town was too small to support even his two hundred followers; a mere Beg, he says, would not think it enough to maintain his retinue. To burden the inhabitants with himself and his small army was out of the question. His first plan was to borrow a village from the Dughlát ruler of Uratipa, and from that centre to subdue some of the mountain strongholds, half-way between Khojend and Samarkand. But this was on his cousin Sultán 'Ali's land, and he soon received peremptory notice to quit. So he buried himself among the Ailák hills, not knowing where to lay his head.

It may seem strange that with so many kinsmen he should have had no refuge to turn to; but, as the Turkish proverb has it, 'Kingship knows no kinship,' and his relations perceived in him a rival more distinctly than a distressed cousin. On the north he had tried his uncle, the Khán, and found him wanting. Sultán 'Ali had forgotten his cousinship in the satisfaction of possessing Samarkánd, which Bábar had won for him. To the east and south the cities were held by the man whom he abhorred above all mankind. This was Khusrau Sháh, a Kipchák Turk, who had been Mahmúd Mirzá's chief minister, and after his master's death did as he pleased with the eastern part of the kingdom, about Hisár and Kunduz, up to the Hindú Kúsh. Other men found Khusrau liberal and generous, but Bábar had an invincible dislike to him. 'Though he prayed regularly,' he writes, 'and abstained from forbidden foods, he was of a black heart and vicious, of mean understanding and slender abilities, a perjured traitor. For the sake of the brief and fleeting pomp of this vain world, he blinded one and murdered another of his benefactor's sons, and made himself accursed of God, abhorred of men, and meet for shame and execration till the day of final retribution.' Khusrau had put out the eyes of Mas'úd, the son of his old master Mahmúd, and after proclaiming another son,

Baisanghar (the same whom Bábar had driven out of Samarkand), king at Hisár, he murdered him; though he had known both the youths from their infancy. 'Every day,' thundered Bábar, 'every day to the day of judgement, may a hundred thousand curses light on the head of the man who plans or does treachery so black; let all who hear of this deed of Khusrau Sháh pour out curses on him; for he who hears of such work and curses not is himself accursed.' Yet, like most tyrants, Khusrau was a coward: Bábar despised him with his whole soul. In spite, he says, of his many and populous dominions, in spite of his army of five thousand men and his ample materials of war, 'he had not the pluck to face a barn-door fowl.' Shaibáni Khán used to say he could frighten Khusrau away with a wave of his hand, 'like a fly from a platter.'

To go to Khusrau was manifestly impossible, and there was no one else left. So Bábar devoured his melancholy among the Ailák shepherds. Whilst he was meditating one day, 'perplexed and distracted with the hopeless state of his affairs,' a holy man, a friend of happier days, but now an exile and wanderer like himself, came and prayed and wept with him. That very afternoon a horseman appeared at the bottom of the valley. He came with a message that brought the prince to his feet in a moment. 'Ali Dost, who had surrendered Andiján to the rebels, and had been rewarded with the government of the important city of Marghinán, sent to pray his sovereign's forgiveness, and offered to deliver up to him the city he governed, and to serve him faithfully till death. His conscience pricked him, and like many another he loved his young king when self-interest did not tempt him too much.

Bábar did not hesitate an instant; no man was more prompt in his decision than this boy of fifteen. It was already sunset, but he started at once. All night and next day till noon he rode without drawing rein; half a day's rest for the horses, and then they were off again at midnight, riding all day till dark; and next morning Marghinán was seen about four miles off. Then for the first time it occurred to him that he had no warranty for 'Ali Dost's good faith: the man 'had stickled at no crime,' and might easily play him false. It was like Bábar to run his head into such a difficulty; he acted first, and thought afterwards. But it was now too late to weigh risks:—'We had passed three days and three nights without rest, and had come a hundred miles without a stop'—a pardonable exaggeration—'neither man nor horse had any strength left; there was no possibility of retreat, nor any refuge to retreat to; having come so far, on we must go. Nothing happens but by God's will.' So on they went, and were rewarded by a loyal welcome from the repentant governor. Bábar and his two hundred and forty men were once more within strong walls. It was the *ποῦ στῶ* that he needed, whence to move the whole kingdom.

The governor of Marghinán was indeed but the

index to a general revulsion of feeling throughout Fargháná. The country was groaning under the tyranny of the rebel Begs, and longed for a prince of the old stock. Even the enemy's soldiers began to desert to Bábar; the hill tribes mustered to his ox-tails; Akhsi itself opened its gates to his officers. In vain the rebels sent a relieving party to hold the citadel of Akhsi. They missed the landing-place in the dusk, and were cut to pieces by the royalists, who stripped their mounts and, plunging bare-back into the river, made short work of the boats. The citadel flew the white flag. On this Andiján also declared for Bábar, in June, 1499; Kásán followed:—Fargháná once more obeyed its lawful king.

The rebellion was scotched, however, not strangled. Bábar had hardly recovered his kingdom when he did as foolish a thing as a restored exile could devise. Among his supporters were some thousands of Mongols, deserters from Tambal, and these men were a constant thorn in his side. They looted the villages, murdered and outraged the peaceful inhabitants, and gave trouble in every way. The people implored the king to deliver them from these scoundrels, and, moved by one of his imprudent impulses, he gave orders that the Mongols should make restitution. The measure would have been practicable only in a settled country with a strong army; but in Fargháná these Mongols were themselves the army, and to coerce them was at that time impossible. The immediate consequence was that four thousand

Mongols mutinied and went over to the rebels. Bábar repented too late. 'It was a senseless thing,' he wrote afterwards, 'to exasperate so many men with arms in their hands. In war and statecraft a thing may seem reasonable at first sight, but it should be weighed and considered in a hundred lights before it is finally decided. This ill-judged order of mine was in fact the ultimate cause of my second expulsion from Andiján.'

Reinforced by these Mongols, Tambal, the rebel leader, took the offensive. Bábar scoured the country to beat up recruits, and collected vast quantities of siege materials, scaling-ladders, *túras* (or siege shields), picks and spades. Tambal twice attacked Andiján, and was beaten off; the king went out in search of him towards Uzkend, and took the fort of Mádu on the way. After this the two armies lay facing each other for a month or more. Bábar made an entrenched camp, protected by a zaríba of brushwood, and posted his vedettes carefully. There were frequent skirmishes, and at last Tambal was forced to give battle. It was the young king's first set field, and he won a slight victory, pursuing and looting the enemy. It could not have been a serious defeat for Tambal, since we find the two forces constantly skirmishing all through the winter. Bábar hutted his troops in cantonments near Núsh-áb, and the excitements of war alternated with the pleasures of the chase. It was 'capital hunting-ground,' he says, 'and good cover for game. Near the river Ilámish, in the jungle, are mountain goats, buck, and wild pig in abundance. In the smaller jungle, scattered in clumps, we found plenty of jungle-fowl and hares. The foxes here are swifter than anywhere else. Whilst in these winter quarters I hunted every two or three days. First we beat up the larger forests for mountain goat and buck, which we chased, and then we hawked in the small jungle for jungle-fowl, or shot them with forked arrows.'

The war, such as it was, grew more and more languid. The king gained no important advantage; his troops grew weary, and insisted on returning home. He had to beat a retreat to Andiján, where he was forced by his officers to accept terms. The kingdom was divided: Bábar was to keep the Andiján bank of the Sir, including Uzkend; and his brother Jahángír, the tool of Tambal, was to hold the Akhsi bank. Prisoners were exchanged, and each retired to his capital.

The fifteenth century had ended disastrously for Bábar. He had lost Samarkand, had been driven into exile, harassed by a powerful rebellion, opposed by his brother, deserted by an army, hampered by discontented officers, and had after all only recovered a part of his kingdom, to hold it at the pleasure of his too powerful nobles. The treaty of the spring of 1500 marks low water in his fortunes; but he had not yet sounded the lowest depths.

CHAPTER IV

Second Conquest of Samarkand

1500–1501

When the two brothers made their treaty in the spring of 1500, there had been a talk of Samarkand, and they had agreed to join in conquering it; after which Bábar consented to make over the whole of Farghána to Jahángír. In his worst straits the memory of the hundred days he had ruled in the capital of his ancestors never faded; the *grande idée* was always in his thoughts; he *would* be King of Samarkand. There was little attraction for him in his present sovereignty at Andiján, with successful rebels in power just across the river, and with 'Ali Dost presuming upon his recent services and playing the king in the very palace. The governor of Andiján, who had once surrendered it to his enemies, thought he had more than atoned for his cowardice by giving the king his own again; and he now acted the master, dismissed Bábar's few trusty followers, and stripped him of all but the name of king. To resist was dangerous, with Tambal over the river ready to step in at the smallest encouragement. 'My case was singularly delicate, and I had to be silent. Many were the humiliations I suffered at that time,' and he was not one to suffer indignities patiently.

An invitation from Samarkand came as a veritable godsend. The great family of the Tarkháns, who had enjoyed special privileges and held high offices for generations, had fallen out with Sultán 'Ali, and had been expelled from Samarkand. They had not forgotten the cheery lad who had been their king for a hundred days, and they offered to help him to recover the throne of Tímúr. The chance of escape from his present humiliations was too good to be even discussed. Bábar set out forthwith (June, 1500), in the absence of his keeper, 'Ali Dost, who, however, caught him up on the way, 'by mere chance and most opportunely,' according to the Memoirs, but one suspects that the Dost was anxious to keep an eye on his protégé. When they reached Uratipa, Kambar 'Ali turned up unexpectedly, 'barefoot and barehead,' having been chased out of his governments by Tambal, in flat violation of the treaty. Bábar cannot suppress a Turki proverb at the expense of his 'muddy-brained' follower. At Yúrat-khán, a little way outside Samarkand, the chief Begs of the city, headed by the Tarkháns, met the king, and did homage. They brought word that Khwája Yahyá was on Bábar's side, and if he co-operated, Samarkand was as good as taken: such was the holy man's reputed influence.

For once, however, it was overrated: Samarkand was not to be surprised this time, and Bábar was forced to retire on Kish, while he saw the great Khán of the Uzbegs enter the coveted city in his stead. Shaibáni had been admitted as an ally, by the influence of its king's mother; but he threw off the disguise as soon as he was inside, insulted the diplomatic dowager, murdered Sultán 'Ali, and thus put an end to the dynasty of Tímúr in the Oxus country. Bábar's comments on his cousin's temporizing policy and punishment are characteristic: 'From over-anxiety to keep this mortal and transitory life, he left a name of infamy behind him; by following the counsels of a woman, he struck himself out of the roll-call of the renowned. Words need not be wasted on such a creature or on such dastardly doings.' The *gravamen* of the offence, however, lay in Sultán 'Ali's preferring Shaibáni to Bábar.

Once more the young adventurer found himself deserted. 'Ali Dost and his people were the first to leave. 'I had taken a rooted dislike to the man,' says the autobiographer, 'and partly from shame, partly for fear, he could not stay with me. He asked leave to go, and I granted it gladly.' A second time they joined the rebel Tambal, and came to an untimely end: the Dost's son verified the proverb about the fate of traitors to their salt; 'the salt caught his eyes,' literally, for he was blinded by the Uzbegs. After the entry of Shaibáni the Samarkand worthies, who had pressed Bábar to come, discarded him, and betook themselves to his bitter enemy Khusrau Sháh at Hisár. The Khwája who had plotted for his success was driven away and murdered by the Uzbegs. The young king was again a wanderer. He could not go back to his own land, where Tambal was now supreme; Hisár and Samarkand were more hostile than ever; and he resolved to seek a refuge once more among the friendly hills of Yár-Ailák. It was no easy journey. First he led his small army up the Kamrúd valley, by dangerous tracks among the rocks, 'and in the steep and narrow ways and gorges which we had to climb, many a horse and camel dropped and fell out. After four or five days we came to the col of Sar-i-Ták. This is a pass—and such a pass! Never did I see one so narrow and steep, or follow paths so toilsome and strait. We pressed on, nevertheless, with incredible labour, through fearful gorges and by tremendous precipices, till, after a hundred agonies and losses, at last we topped those murderous steep defiles, and came down on the borders of Kán, with its lovely expanse of lake,' all the more lovely and peaceful to Bábar's appreciative eyes after the horrid gloom of the mountain passes. Thence the banks of the Kohik led him to the Ailáks.

Even now, he was not discouraged. He was a born soldier of fortune, and so long as he had a few hundred men at his back he was ready for any adventure. A short rest, a consultation with his Begs, and he was again on the march for Samarkand. Mad as the project seemed, he had good reasons for the attack. If ever the imperial city was to be his, it must be before Shaibáni had time to establish his power. At present he was newly arrived; he had murdered the king, disgraced and banished the holy man, and must be detested by the inhabitants. He must not be given time to overcome their dislike; he must not be allowed to take root. Fortunately he was encamped outside the city. If only Bábar could get into Samarkand by a surprise, he was confident that the citizens would rally to his cause—to any cause but the Uzbegs. 'At all events,' he said, in his happy-go-lucky way, 'when once the city is taken, God's will be done.' The first attempt failed: they rode all day and reached Yúrat-Khán at midnight, only to find the garrison of Samarkand on the alert. Then, about November, acting on an auspicious dream, Bábar tried again. This time the saintly Khwája 'Abd-al-Makárim rode beside him, and they made a rapid dash for Samarkand. Fourscore of his best men scaled the wall opposite 'the Lover's Cave,' and seizing the Firúza Gate threw it open just as Bábar galloped up with the main force. 'The city was asleep: only some shop-keepers, peeping out, discovered what had happened, and gave thanks to God. Soon the news spread, and the citizens with great joy and congratulations fraternized with my men. They chased the Uzbegs in every street and corner, hunting them down and killing them like mad dogs.'

The city was won—won by a handful of two hundred and forty men. Bábar took his seat under the great arch, and the people came to acclaim him, and (what he needed even more) brought him food. Then he mounted and rode pell-mell to the Iron Gate, where the Uzbegs were reported to be making a stand. The rabble, however, had done the business, and the enemy were flying for their lives. Just at this moment Shaibáni himself rode up from his camp outside the city, with an escort of a hundred horse. 'It was a splendid opportunity,' says Bábar, 'but I had only a handful of men with me'; and so Shaibáni got safely away, to work much mischief against him in years to come. But it was no time for forebodings, and Bábar gave himself up to the intoxication of success. He was welcomed to his heart's content: never was triumph more popular; the city was *en fête*, and the great men, nobles, and dignitaries came out and waited on his Majesty as he sat enthroned in the beautiful Garden Palace. 'For almost one hundred and forty years Samarkand had been the capital of my family. A foreign robber, coming the Lord knows whence, had seized the sceptre that dropped from our hands. God most High now restored it, and gave me back my plundered desolated land.'

They made a chronogram for the event, in the approved Oriental style:—

> Tell me, my soul, what is the year?
> Bábar Bahádur is conqueror here.

The letters in *Fátiḥ Bábar Bahádur*, taken as numbers, spell 906, the year of the Hijra in which

Bábar conquered Samarkand, or 1500 A.D. To add to his happiness, his mother and other women relations joined him. They had followed him from Andiján, and suffered great privations; but now all was well. The little 'Áïsha, to whom he was betrothed when a child, had become his wife at Khojend 'during the troubles,' and at Samarkand she gave birth to his first child: they called the baby Fakhr-an-Nisá, the 'glory of her sex,' but 'in a month or forty days she went to partake of the mercy of God.' Bábar was then just nineteen[1], and he makes the odd confession, especially curious in an Eastern, that so far he had 'never conceived a passion for any woman, and indeed had never been so placed as even to hear or witness words of love or amorous discourse.' He admits that he did not love 'Áïsha, and she had therefore a fair excuse when she afterwards left him. Later on he fell really in love with her youngest sister; but, so far as the records go, Bábar seems to have been singularly insusceptible to the tender passion; though—or because—no one was more attached to the women of his own blood, or more deferential to women in general. He had, however, a dread of a shrew, which may have been rooted in some marital experience. 'May Almighty God,' he fervently exclaims, 'preserve all good Muslims from such a visitation, and may no such thing as

[1] So he says, reckoning by lunar years; if so, the child was born in July, 1501, just before Bábar left Samarkand. He was under eighteen (*solar* years) when he conquered it.

an ill-tempered cross-grained wife be left in the world!'

The first step of the new King of Samarkand was to cultivate, as we should say, 'foreign relations.' He sent embassies to the neighbouring rulers, inviting their friendship and support against the growing power of the Uzbegs. The missions were a failure; some refused all co-operation, others put him off with cold answers; his brother Jahángír, now King of Farghána, sent a paltry hundred men; the Khán, his uncle, furnished a few hundred more; Sultán Husain Mirzá of Herát, the most powerful representative of Tímúr's line, sent never a sword. Bábar consoled himself now and then by 'composing a couplet or two, but did not venture on a complete ode.' In more practical moods he looked to the efficiency of his army, which was rapidly increasing. Most of the towns and villages of the province of Samarkand had fallen into his hands, and fresh levies came trooping in. Some of the Tarkhán nobles, too, returned to him, and by May, 1501, he was in a condition to take the field against Shaibáni.

The Uzbeg leader had retired to Bukhárá after Bábar's unexpected arrival at Samarkand, but he was now at Dabúsi, within striking distance, and Bábar marched out to the Bridge Head (*Sar-i-púl*) to meet him. As before, he formed an entrenched zaríba, and so long as he kept behind his defences Shaibáni could not touch him. In an evil moment, however, the stars in their courses hurried on an engagement.

It happened that the Eight Stars [of the Great Bear?] were exactly between the two armies, whereas for the next fortnight they would be on the enemy's side. In his after wisdom Bábar confesses that 'these observations were idle, and there was no excuse for my haste'; but at the moment the Eight Stars persuaded him, and without waiting for the reinforcements which the Tarkháns and Dughlát Amírs were bringing to his support, the superstitious prince gave battle.

Early on the May morning the troops of Samarkand, man and horse armed in mail, marched out of their entrenchments. The enemy was drawn up ready for them. Shaibáni had the longer line, for he quickly turned Bábar's left, and wheeled upon his rear. This was the usual Uzbeg tactic or *tulughma*: first turning the enemy's flank, then charging simultaneously on front and rear, letting fly their arrows at a breakneck gallop, and if repulsed retiring at top speed. Bábar was evidently unprepared for it at the battle of Sar-i-púl, though he learnt to use it with deadly effect in later years in India. His rear indeed changed front, under fire, but so clumsily that the right became separated in the movement; and, although the enemy's front attack was driven back on his centre, Bábar was out of touch with his right, his left was already routed, and his rear hotly engaged. To add to the confusion, his Mongol troopers, instead of fighting, fell to unhorsing and looting their own side. 'Such is the way of those Mongol rascals: if they win, they seize the booty; if they are beaten, they unhorse and plunder their own allies, and carry off the spoil all the same.' Surrounded and attacked on all sides, by friends and foes alike, with the arrows dropping in from all points of the compass, Bábar's followers broke and fled, and he found himself on the river bank with only ten or fifteen men. The Kohik had to be crossed, and it was out of their depth, but they plunged in, horse and all, heavily armed at all points as they were, and swam across; then, cutting away their horses' heavy trappings and mail, they rode for their lives. As they went they could see their Mongols stripping and murdering their dismounted comrades: Bábar's scorn breaks out in verse:—

> Were the Mongols a race of angels, it would still be a vile nation;
> Were their name written in gold, it would be abomination.
> Beware you pluck not a single ear from a Mongol field,
> For whatever is sown with Mongol seed has an odious yield.

He reached Samarkand, but without an army. Six valiant Begs had fallen, the rest had vanished. He had to defend the city with the help of a loyal but untrained mob, led by a remnant of his dejected followers. In those days, however, strong walls counted for much against even an overpowering superiority in numbers and discipline, and for seven months Bábar held out against Shaibáni's host. The rabble stood by him pluckily, and even ventured out to skirmish with the enemy, covered by a brisk discharge from the crossbows over the gates. Once, under cover of a feigned assault, the Uzbegs got a footing on the wall by the Needlemakers' Gate: but the sturdy townsmen discovered them, and cut them down as they climbed up on their tall ladders. The nights were made horrible by the din of Shaibáni's big drums, which were beaten loudly before the gate, accompanied by shouts and alarums. Matters could not go on for ever like this. There was no sign of relief.

> 'Though I had sent ambassadors and messengers to all the princes and chiefs round about, no help came from any. Indeed, when I was at the height of my power, and had suffered as yet neither defeat nor loss, I had received no help, and could hardly expect it now that I was reduced to such distress. To draw out the siege in hopes of any succour from them was clearly useless. The ancients have said that to hold a fortress, a head, two hands, and two feet are needed. The head is a captain, the two hands are two friendly forces advancing from different sides, the two feet are water and food in the fort.'

In this case the head had to act by itself; the friendly hands were not stretched out, and the feet were all but exhausted. There was no corn in Samarkand; the poor were eating dogs and donkeys; the horses were browsing on the branches of trees; people were secretly escaping over the walls. There was nothing for it but surrender, and Bábar capitulated—so he puts it—one can hardly expect him to confess the bald fact, but it is more truthful to say that he fled. His mother and two other ladies escaped with him, but his eldest sister fell into the hands of

Shaibáni and entered his harím; evidently she was part of the capitulation[1].

One would think that nothing could be much more depressing than this midnight exodus from the city of his ambition, which he had twice held and twice lost again, but Bábar's spirits were extraordinarily elastic; and after a night spent in losing himself and his unfortunate companions in the tangle of the canals, when at the time of morning prayers they at last found their road, we find the desolate exile and his 'muddy-brained' follower indulging in a breakneck gallop. Bábar relates it as if it were the sort of amusement that dethroned monarchs usually pursued:—

'On the road I had a race with Kambar 'Ali and Kásim Beg. My horse got the lead. As I turned round on my seat to see how far I had left them behind, my saddle turned, the girth being slack, and I fell right on my head. Though I sprang up at once and mounted, I did not recover the full possession of my senses till the evening, and the world and all that happened then passed before my eyes like a dream or phantasy and disappeared. The time of afternoon prayers was past before we reached Ilán-útí, where we dismounted, and killing a horse, butchered him and cooked slices of his flesh. We stayed a little time to rest our horses, then remounted and reached the village of Khalíla before day-break: thence to Dizak. . . . Here we found nice fat flesh, bread of fine flour well baked, sweet melons, and excellent

[1] This is clearly stated in the *Shaibáni-náma*, xxxix; but it seems the lady was in love with the brave barbarian, who, however, soon divorced her.

grapes in great abundance: thus passing from the extreme of famine to plenty, and from a state of danger and calamity to peace and ease.

> From famine and distress we have escaped to repose;
> We have gained fresh life and a fresh world.
> The fear of death was removed from the heart;
> The torments of hunger were taken away[1].

In all my life I never enjoyed myself so much or felt at any time so keenly the pleasures of peace and plenty. Enjoyment after suffering, abundance after want, come with increased relish and afford more exquisite delight. I have four or five times in the course of my life passed thus from distress to ease and from suffering to enjoyment; but this was the first time I had ever been delivered from the assaults of my enemy and the pressure of hunger, and thence passed to the ease of safety and the joy of plenty.'

[1] In the original the first two lines are in Turki, the last two in Persian.

CHAPTER V

Exile

1502

Bábar did not see Samarkand again for many years. He had matched his strength against Shaibáni Khán, and the Uzbeg had shown himself the stronger. The young prince—he was king of nothing now—did not give in on that account; he sought more than once to cross swords with his powerful adversary; but he made no fresh attempt upon his capital for a long while. For the present he retired among the shepherds on the hills near Uratipa, waiting upon events. He had the happy faculty of being interested wherever he was, and now he found much amusement in talking to the Persian Sarts in the mountain village, and watching their sheep and herds of mares, as he took long rambles barefooted among the pastures. He lodged with the headman of the village, a veteran of seventy or eighty, whose mother was still alive at the age of a hundred and eleven. She had children, grandchildren, great-grandchildren, and great-great-grandchildren to the number of ninety-six in the district round about, and she delighted the prince with her reminiscences of old days. One of her people had actually served in Tímúr's army when he invaded Hindústán: 'she remembered it well, and often told us stories about it[1].' Perhaps the old woman's tales fired her listener's imagination, and led him to dream of that Indian empire which was one day to lie at his feet.

At present nothing lay at his feet but humble peasants and their flocks. He was so poor that he viewed with alarm the arrival of his grandmother, 'with the family and heavy baggage, and a few lean hungry followers,' escaped from Samarkand. His pride had fallen so low that he was persuaded by a politic counsellor to send a present to his more fortunate brother Jahángír: he sent him an ermine cap, and unwillingly added a heavy Samarkand sword for his old enemy Tambal. He lived to regret the sword. The presents were carried by those of his followers who, having nothing but mischief to do in the village, were allowed to return to their homes at Andiján. He made a raid himself in the winter. Shaibáni was ravaging the country about the Sir, and Bábar could not resist the temptation of having a thrust at him. He led his few troopers to Panjkend, but found nothing of the Uzbegs but their tracks. The river was another temptation, for Bábar was a magnificent swimmer, as he afterwards proved in India.

[1] As Tímúr invaded India in 1398, the old woman was a child of seven at the time; but her recollection was doubtless refreshed in after years by the returned warrior.

'It was terribly cold,' he writes, 'and the wind from the desert had lost nothing of its violence and blew keen: so cold was it that in a few days we lost several comrades from its nip. I had to bathe, for religious purification, and went down to a stream that was frozen at the banks but not in the middle, by reason of the swift current. I plunged in, and dived sixteen times, but the biting chill of the water cut through me.'

Another fruitless expedition followed, and then Bábar seriously considered his prospects. He reflected that 'to ramble thus from hill to hill, without house or home, country or resting-place, could serve no good purpose.' His only plan was to go to the Khán his uncle. On June 16, 1502, he kept the great festival, the 'Id-i-Kurbán, at Sháhrukhíya, and then went straight to Táshkend. Mahmúd Khán welcomed him with the hospitality of the desert, but evidently without much sympathy. When Bábar presented him with an elegant quatrain on the miseries of exile, the Khán would not commit himself on the subject: 'it was pretty evident that he had no great skill in poetic diction,' said the mortified poet, but it is also possible that the uncle thought his nephew had brought his misfortunes on his own head. The Memoirs give many curious pictures of Mongol customs, and show the character of the people from whom Bábar drew at least half his blood.

During his stay with his uncle at Táshkend, the restless Khán took a desire to lead his Mongols against Tambal, who was harassing Uratipa. The army marched to Panjkend, where Bábar assisted in the ceremony of trooping the colours according to Mongol traditions. First the Khán dismounted, and nine ox-tail standards[1] were set before him. A Mongol stood by, holding in his hand an ox's shank-bone, to which he tied a long white cotton cloth. Another fastened three long slips of white cloth below the horse-tail of the standard.

'One corner of one of the cloths the Khán took, and putting it beneath his feet, stood upon it. I stood on a corner of another of the long slips, which was in like manner tied under one of the ox-tails; and Sultán Muhammed Khanikeh [the Khán's son] took the third, and placing the cloth under his feet, likewise stood upon a corner of it. Then the Mongol who had tied the cloths, holding the ox-shank in his hand, made a speech in the Mongol tongue, looking often to the standards, and pointing and making signs towards them. The Khán and all the men formed in line, took *kúmis* in their hands, and sprinkled it towards the standards. All the trumpets and drums struck up at once, and all the soldiers who were drawn up shouted the war-cry. These ceremonies they repeated thrice.'

All this was minutely regulated by precedent, for 'among the Mongols, the rules of Chingiz Kaán are still strictly observed. Each man has his appointed post; those appointed to the right or left wing or centre have their established posts handed down from

[1] The *tug* or standard of the Mongols was made of the tail of a mountain ox. There is an admirable painting of this ceremony in the sixteenth-century Persian MS. of Bábar's Memoirs preserved in the British Museum (Or. 3,714).

father to son; and those of the greatest trust and rank are at the extremities or flanks.'

After this review, the army marked out a great hunting circle, and hunted as far as the Chahár-Bágh of Burk. Meanwhile Bábar indulged his poetry and melancholy by composing his first *ghazal* or ode, beginning—

> I have found in the world no faithful friend but my soul;
> Save mine own heart I have no trusty confidant.

They then marched to the Sir, where the young prince gave the officers a banquet, at which, in true Mongol style, the gold clasp of his girdle was stolen. Some of the Begs deserted to Tambal next day—with the gold clasp, as Bábar suspected. He was out of humour with everything, even with making war: 'this expedition of the Khán' (he says) 'was rather a useless sort of excursion. He took no fort; he beat no enemy; he went and came back again.'

Inaction and dependence did not agree with Bábar's proud and energetic spirit.

'While I remained at Táshkend,' he confesses, 'I endured great distress and misery. I had no country nor hopes of one. Most of my servants had left me out of sheer want; the few who still stood by me could not escort me on my journeys for want of means. When I went to my uncle the Khán's audience, I was attended only by one or two; fortunately this did not happen among strangers, but with my own kindred. After paying my respects to the Khán, my uncle, I went in to wait on [his mother] the Sháh Begum, bareheaded and barefoot, as freely as one might do in one's own home. But at last I was worn out with this unsettled state, with no house or home, and weary of life. I said to myself, rather than pass my life in such wretchedness and misery, it were better to go my way and hide me in some nook where I might be unknown and undistinguished —to flee away from the sight of man as far as my feet could carry me.'

He thought of China, which he had always longed to visit, and now that he had no ties of kingship, and his family was in safety with the Khán, he resolved to journey into the unknown. His plan was to go and visit his younger uncle, Ahmad Khán, surnamed Aláchá or 'the Slayer,' in Mongolistán, and thence escape to the eastward. But the plan was upset by the unexpected tidings that Ahmad was actually coming to visit his brother Mahmúd, whom he had not seen for a quarter of a century—indeed they had been on no friendly terms. Bábar set out at once to welcome him, and it happened that the meeting between uncle and nephew took place quite suddenly.

'All at once I found myself face to face with him. I instantly dismounted and went forward to meet him. The Khán, seeing me get off, was much upset. He had meant to dismount somewhere and receive me, seated, with all the ceremonies; but I had come upon him too quickly, and dismounted in such a hurry, that there was no time for etiquette. The moment I sprang from my horse, I knelt down and then embraced my uncle. He was a good deal agitated and disconcerted.'

However, on the morrow, 'the Slayer' had his wish, and carried out the formalities. He sent Bábar a complete Mongol dress, and one of his own horses ready saddled. 'The dress consisted of a Mongol cap embroidered with gold thread, a long frock of China satin adorned with flowered needlework, a Chinese belt of the old style, with whetstone and purse-pocket, to which were hung three or four things like the trinkets women wear at their necks, such as a perfume box and little bag.' They journeyed together to Táshkend, and the elder Khán came out a dozen miles to meet his brother. Then he awaited him, seated solemnly under a tent.

'The younger Khán went straight up, and on coming near him in front, turned off to the left, and fetched a circle round him, till he was again in front, when he dismounted, and advancing to the proper distance for the *kornish* obeisance, bowed nine times, and then came up and embraced him. The elder Khán on his approach stood up for the embrace; they stood a long time clasped in each other's arms. Then the younger Khán, on retiring, again bowed nine times; and when he presented his *pishkash* (or tributary offering) he bent again many times, after which they both sat down. All the younger Khán's men were dressed in the Mongol fashion, with the native caps and flowered China satin frocks; their quivers and saddles were of shagreen, and their horses were decked and caparisoned in a singular fashion. The younger Khán came with but few followers—less than two thousand. He was a stout, courageous man, and a perfect master of the sabre, his favourite weapon. He used to say that the mace, javelin, and battle-axe, if they hit, could only be relied on for a single blow. This sharp, trusty sword he never allowed to be away from him; it was always either at his waist or in his hand. As he had been brought up in an out-of-the-way country, he was something rude of manner and uncouth of speech.'

The two Kháns, joining their forces, celebrated their reunion by a warlike expedition. Tambal must be crushed. He was then at Andiján, and thither they advanced against him (July, 1502), sending Bábar with a detachment to move upon Ush and Uzkend, and thus take the enemy in the rear. He took Ush by surprise, to the delight of the inhabitants, who dreaded Tambal; and the 'Ils and Ulúses,' or wandering tribes, flocked to his standard. Uzkend and Marghinán declared for their former king, with all the country on the southern side of the Sir, save Andiján itself. Meanwhile Tambal lay unperturbed between Akhsi and Karmán, facing the Kháns, in his entrenched zaríba. Bábar bethought him of a night reconnaissance to Andiján, where the citizens at least were understood to be loyal. He set out one evening from Ush, and at midnight was within a couple of miles of the capital. Then he sent forward Kambar 'Ali with a party to open a secret conference with the Khwájas and leading men. Bábar himself waited their return, seated on horseback with the rest of his men. He must tell the story himself:—

'It might be about the end of the third watch of the night, some of us were nodding, others fast asleep, when all at once kettle-drums struck up, accompanied by warlike shout and hubbub. My men being off their guard and oppressed with drowsiness, not knowing how many or how few the enemy might be, were seized with panic and took to disorderly flight. I had no time to rally them, but advanced towards the enemy, accompanied by Mír Sháh Kochín, Bábá Shírzád, and Dost Násir. Except us four, all ran off to a man. We had gone but a little way when the enemy, after discharging a flight of arrows, raised the war-cry, and charged upon us. One fellow on a horse with a white blaze came up to me. I let fly an arrow which hit the horse, and he instantly fell dead. The others drew rein a little. My three companions said, "The night is dark, and it is impossible to judge the number and force of the enemy; all our troops are fled; we are but four, and with such a number how can we hope to win? Let us follow our party, rally them, and bring them back into action." So we galloped off and overtook our men, but in vain we flogged them—we could not make them stand anyhow. Again we four turned and gave the pursuers a flight of arrows. They halted a space; but after one or two volleys they saw we were only four, and set off again in pursuit of our men, to strike and unhorse them. Three or four times we covered and protected our people in this way, and as they would not rally, I was constantly turning with my three companions to keep the enemy in check and bring them up short with our arrows.'

They kept up the pursuit, nevertheless, for the space of five miles, till they came to some hills, when Bábar saw how few they were, and cried out, 'Come, let us charge them.' When they charged, the others stood still! And they proved to be some of their Mongol allies, who had mistaken them in the dark for the enemy. After this confusion the reconnaissance naturally failed, and all returned abashed to Ush.

Nevertheless Tambal became disheartened: the people were going back to their old allegiance, and he felt he must soon break up his force and retire. Bábar, discovering this downheartedness, forthwith marched again upon Andiján, met a body of the enemy outside, and drove them in; but was dissuaded by his old Begs from forcing an entrance in the dark: 'Had we done so,' he remarked afterwards, 'there is not the shadow of a doubt that the place would have fallen into our hands.' As it was, while negligently sleeping in the open plain, without pickets or sentries, they were surprised at dawn by the main body under Tambal himself:—

'Kambar 'Ali galloped up, shouting, "The enemy are upon us—rouse up!" Having so said, without a moment's halt he rode on to give the alarm. I had gone to sleep, as my custom was even in times of security, without taking off my *jáma*, and instantly arose, girt on my sabre and quiver, and mounted my horse. My standard-bearer seized the standard-pole, but had no time to tie on the ox-tail; so seizing the staff as it was, he leapt on horseback, and we went towards the quarter whence the enemy were advancing. When I mounted there were ten or fifteen men with me. By the time I had advanced a bow-shot we fell in with the enemy's skirmishers. At this moment there might be about ten men with me. Riding quickly up to them and shooting our arrows, we came upon the foremost, smote them and drove them back, and pressing on pursued them for another bow-shot, when we fell in with the main body of the enemy. Sultán Ahmad Tambal was standing there [in front of his troops] with about a hundred men; he was speaking with another man in front of the line, and in the act of saying, "Smite them! Smite them!" but his men were sidling in a hesitating way, as if saying, "Shall we flee? Let us flee!" yet without budging.

'There were now only three men left with me—Dost Násir, Mirzá Kúli Kukildásh, and Kerímdád Khodáidád the Turkmán. One arrow was on my notch and I shot it point blank at Tambal's helmet. Again I felt the quiver, and brought out a barbed arrow, which my uncle the Khán had given me. Unwilling to throw it away, I returned it, and thus lost time. Then I put another arrow on the string and went forward, the others lagging a little behind. Two men came straight on to meet me, the forwarder was Tambal. There was a causeway between us. He mounted on one side of it just as I mounted on the other, and we met so that my right hand was towards my enemy and Tambal's right towards me. Except for his horse, Tambal was completely in mail. I had on my cuirass, and carried my sabre and bow and arrows. I drew up to my ear and sent my arrow right at his head, when at the same instant an arrow struck me on the right thigh and pierced through and through. Tambal rushed on, and, with the great Samarkand sword I had given him, smote me such a blow on my steel headpiece as to stun me. Though not a link of the cap was cut, my head was severely bruised. I had neglected to clean my sword, so that it was rusty, and I lost time in drawing it.

'I was alone, solitary, in the midst of foes. It was no time for standing still, so I turned my bridle, receiving another sabre stroke on my quiver. I had gone back seven or eight paces when three foot-soldiers came up and joined me. Tambal attacked Dost Násir with the sword. They followed us about a bow-shot. . . . God directed us aright, so that we came exactly upon one of the fords of the river. Just after crossing, Dost Násir's horse fell from exhaustion. We halted to remount him, and passing among the hills got back to Ush safely[1].'

The behaviour of his two uncles now began to make him uneasy. Mahmúd Khán very coolly made over to his brother all the places which Bábar had reconquered of his patrimony, on the ground that Ahmad Khán required a good position close at hand in order to withstand Shaibáni. They would presently conquer Samarkand, and Bábar should have that in exchange for Farghána. He was not deceived; it was not the first time that his uncle had coveted the little kingdom. 'Probably,' he wrote, 'all this talk was merely to overreach me, and had they succeeded, they would have forgotten their promise. But there was no help for it: willing or not, I had to seem content.' He went to visit his younger uncle, who seeing him walking painfully with a stick, by reason of his wound, ran out beyond the tent-ropes and embraced him heartily, saying, 'Brother, you have quitted yourself like a hero.' The visitor noticed that the tent was small and untidy: melons, grapes, and stable furniture were lying about in a muddle. The Khán, however, was kind, and at once sent his own surgeon to dress the wound.

'He was wonderfully skilful in his art,' says Bábar, in all good faith. 'If a man's brains had come out he could cure him, and he could even easily heal severed arteries. To some wounds he applied plasters; for others he prescribed

[1] A few words have been added from Bábar's second account of this adventure (pp. 265-6 of Erskine's translation).

doses. To my thigh wound he applied the skin of some fruits which he had prepared and dried, and he did not insert a seton. He also once gave me something like a vein to eat. He told me that "a man once had his leg broken so that part of the bone as large as one's hand was completely shattered. I cut open the integuments, extracted the whole of the shattered bone, and inserted in its place a pulverised preparation, which grew in place of the bone, *and became bone itself*, and the leg was perfectly cured." He told me many similar strange and wonderful stories of cures, such as the surgeons of our parts are totally unable to effect.'

No doubt this extraordinary operator made a good cure of the wound in the thigh, for we find his patient soon afterwards riding to Akhsi, at the invitation of Tambal's younger brother, Shaikh Báyazíd. This strange partnership led to many adventures.

CHAPTER VI

FLIGHT

1502–1503

THE motive of Tambal's brother in inviting Bábar to join him was obvious enough. Bábar was the only capable commander on the side of the two Kháns; if he could be detached, the Mongol invasion of Farghána would probably fall to pieces; and once in Tambal's power, the young king would doubtless be cured for ever of all ambition. Yet something might be made of the proposal. His two uncles suggested that he should take advantage of his new ally's cordiality, and entrap him; but treachery was the thing of all others he despised: 'Such trickery and underhandedness were altogether against my grain and nature; besides, there must be a treaty, and I could never bring myself to break my word.' Nevertheless, he would try to win over Báyazíd to his side, and thus make a split in Tambal's party.

All went well at first. He arrived at Akhsi, and took up his quarters in the stone fort where his father's old palace stood. Báyazíd seemed really loyal, though he kept the command of the castle. Presently news came that Shaibáni was on the march, and that the two Kháns had immediately beaten a retreat. Bábar was thus deserted, and the next thing was the approach of Tambal at the head of two or three thousand men-at-arms. The trap was on the point of snapping; the brothers' plans had worked out beautifully. With his usual carelessness, or want of suspicion, Bábar had not thought of seizing the castle, the key of the position, nor had he even set a guard at the bridge by which Tambal must cross. His own followers were dispersed all over the country, and he had but a hundred left. To hold the town without securing the castle was hopeless; yet Bábar attempted it with the help of his brother Jahángír, who had at last fled from his gaoler. Flight was the only chance of safety, and the story of how Bábar made his escape, and how he fared on his wild journey, fills some exciting pages of the Memoirs:—

'We had no sooner come opposite the gate than we saw Shaikh Báyazíd, with a quilted gambeson over his vest; he had just then entered the gateway with three or four horsemen, and was riding into the town. . . . I immediately drew to the head the arrow that was in my notch, and let him have it full. It only grazed his neck, but it was a fine shot. The moment he had traversed the gate he turned short to the right and fled in a panic down a narrow lane. I pursued. Kúli Kukildásh struck down one foot-soldier with his mace, and had passed another, when the fellow aimed an arrow at Ibráhím Beg, who baulked him by shouting "Hai! Hai!" and went on; but the man, being no further off than the porch from the hall, let fly an arrow which hit me under the arm. I had on a Kálmak mail, and two of its plates were pierced and shivered by the shot. Then he fled and I sent an arrow after him, which caught a foot-soldier who happened just then to be flying along the rampart, and pinned his cap to the wall, where it stuck transfixed, dangling from the parapet. He took his turban, twisted it round his arm, and ran off. A man on horseback passed close to me, rushing up the narrow lane. I gave him the point of my sword on the temple; he swerved over as if to fall, but caught the wall, and thus supported recovered his seat and escaped.

'Having scattered all the horse and foot that were at the gate, we took possession of it. There was now no reasonable chance of success, for they had two or three thousand well-armed men in the citadel, while I had only a hundred, or at most two hundred, in the outer stone fort; and besides, about as long before this as milk takes to boil, Jahángír Mirzá had been beaten and driven out, and half my men with him. Yet such was my inexperience that, posting myself in the gateway, I sent a messenger to Jahángír to bid him join me in another effort. But in truth the business was over... We continued waiting at the gate for the return of my messenger. He came and told us that Jahángír was already gone some time. It was no season for tarrying, and we too set off: indeed my staying so long was very unwise. Only twenty or thirty men now remained with me. The moment we moved off a strong troop of the enemy came smartly after us; we just cleared the drawbridge as they reached its town end. Banda 'Ali Beg called out to Ibráhím Beg, "You are always boasting and bragging: stop and let us exchange a few sword-cuts." Ibráhím, who was close to me, answered, "Come on, then; what lets you?" Senseless madcaps, to bandy pretensions at such a moment! It was no time for a trial of skill, or any sort of delay. We made off at our top speed, the enemy at our heels. They brought down man after man as they gained on us.

'Within a couple of miles of Akhsi there is a place called the Garden-Dome. We had just passed it when Ibráhím Beg called loudly to me for help. I looked round and saw him engaged with a home-bred slave of Shaikh Báyazíd. I turned at once to go back, when Ján Kúli and Biyán Kúli, who rode beside me, seized my rein and hurried me on, saying, "What time is this for turning back?" Before we reached Sang (three miles from Akhsi) they had unhorsed most of my followers; but after Sang we saw no more pursuers. We followed the river of Sang, being then only eight men. A sort of defile leads up stream among broken glens, far from the beaten track. By this unfrequented path we went, till leaving the river on the right we struck into another narrow track. It was about afternoon prayers when we came out from the glens upon the level country. There we saw a black spot far off on the plain. I put my men under cover, and crept up a hillock on foot to spy what it might be; when suddenly a number of horsemen galloped up behind us: we could not tell how many there were, but took to our horses and fled. The horsemen who followed us (I afterwards learnt) were not above twenty or twenty-five in all, and we were eight. Had we but known their number at first we should have given them warm work, but we thought they were in force; and so we continued our flight. The truth is that the pursued are no match for the pursuers, even though numbers be in their favour, for

A single shout is enough to finish the vanquished.

'Ján Kúli said, "We cannot go on like this; they will take us all. Do you and the foster-brother (Kukildásh) take the two best horses of the party and galloping together keep the spare horses on your bridle; perhaps you may escape."

The advice was good, but I could not leave my followers dismounted in presence of the enemy. At last my party began to separate and drop behind. My own horse began to flag. Ján Kúli dismounted and gave me his. I leapt down and mounted his horse, and he mounted mine. At this instant Shahím Násir and 'Abd-al-Kaddús, who had fallen behind, were unhorsed by the enemy. Ján Kúli also dropped behind, but it was no time to try to shield or help him. We pushed our horses to their utmost stretch, but they gradually flagged and slacked. Dost Beg's horse was done up and dropped behind, and mine began to give signs of being worn out. Kambar 'Ali dismounted and gave me his horse. He mounted mine, and presently fell behind. Khwája Husaini, who was lame, turned aside to the heights. I was left alone with Mirzá Kúli Kukildásh.

'Our horses were past galloping; we went on at a canter, but Kúli's horse went slower and slower. I said, "If I lose you, whither can I go? Dead or alive we will keep together." I held on my way, turning from time to time to watch him. At last he said, "My horse is utterly blown, and you cannot escape encumbered with me. Push on and shift for yourself; perchance you may still escape." I was in a horrible situation. Kúli then fell behind, too, and I was alone. Two of the enemy were in sight . . . they gained on me; my horse flagged. There was a hill about a couple of miles off, and I came up to a heap of stones. My horse was done up, I considered, and the hill yet a considerable way ahead. What was to be done? I had still about twenty arrows in my quiver. Should I dismount at this heap of stones, and hold my ground as long as my arrows lasted? But then it struck me I might yet be able to win the hill, and if I did I could stick a few arrows in my belt and manage to climb it. I had great faith in my own nimbleness. So I kept on my course. My horse could make no speed, and my pursuers got within bowshot of me; but I was sparing of my arrows and did not shoot. They too were chary, and came no nearer than a bowshot, but kept tracking me.

'I drew near the hill about sunset, when they suddenly called out to me, "Where are you going, that you fly in this manner? Jahángír Mirzá has been taken and brought in, and Násir Mirzá has been seized." I was greatly alarmed at these words, for if all [three] of us fell into their hands, we had everything to dread! I made no answer, but kept on for the hill. When we had gone a little further they called to me again, speaking more graciously, and dismounting from their horses to address me. I paid no attention, but kept on my way, and entering a gorge, began to ascend it, and went on until about bedtime prayers, when I reached a rock as big as a house. I went behind it, and found an ascent of steep ledges where the horse could not keep his footing. They also dismounted, and began to address me still more courteously and respectfully, expostulating, and saying, "What end can it serve to go on thus in a dark night, where there is no road? Where can you possibly go?" They both solemnly swore that "Sultán Ahmad Beg [Tambal] wishes to put you on the throne."

'I answered, "I can put no trust in anything of the sort, nor could I possibly join him. If you really wish to do me an important service, you have now an opportunity which may not recur for years. Point me out a road by which I may rejoin the Kháns, and I will show you kindness and favour beyond your utmost desire. If you will not, then return the way you came, and leave me to accomplish my fate—even that will be no slight service." "Would to God," they exclaimed, "that we had never come; but as we are here, how can we desert you in this desolate situation? Since you will not accompany us to Tambal, we shall follow and serve you, go where you will." I said, "Swear then to me by the Holy Book that you are sincere in your offer." And they swore that tremendous oath. I now began to have some confidence in them, and said, "An open road was once pointed out to me near this same valley: do you proceed by it." Though they had sworn, yet I could not thoroughly trust them, so I made them go on in front, and I followed them.'

So they journeyed on, the fugitive king and his two doubtful guides. They were misleading him, of course, and meant to deliver him up to Tambal. They got him some bread, however, for starving was no part of their plan, and, 'each with a loaf under his arm,' the three sat munching on a hillock, keeping watch on all sides and on each other. They saw people passing below, whom they knew, but Bábar dared not trust himself to them, though he trusted his two strange companions even less. It was now afternoon of the second day, and they went down to graze their famished horses in the marshy valley. Here they encountered the headman of the neighbouring village of Karmán, and Bábar knew him, and spoke him fair, and tried to secure his fidelity and help. At night they again descended from their rock, and the men gave Bábar an old cloak of lambskin, with the wool inside and coarse cloth without, for it was winter and bitterly cold. They brought him also a mess of boiled millet flour, which he found 'wonderfully comforting.' They were waiting (they said), to see the headman again; but 'those misbegotten treacherous clowns' had meanwhile sent a messenger to Tambal to betray Bábar's retreat.

'Entering a stone house and kindling a fire, I closed my eyes for a moment in sleep. These crafty fellows pretended a vast anxiety to serve me: "We must not stir from this neighbourhood," said they, "till we have news of Kádir Berdi [the headman]. The room where we are, however, is in the midst of houses. There is a place on the outskirts where we could be quite unsuspected, could we but reach it." So we mounted our horses about midnight and went to a garden on the outskirts of the suburbs. Bábá Sairámi watched on the terrace roof of the house, keeping a sharp look-out in every direction.

'It was near noon [on the third day of the flight] when he came down from the terrace and said to me, "Here comes Yúsuf the constable." I was seized with prodigious alarm, and said, "Find out if he comes in consequence of knowing that I am here." Bábá went out, and after some talk returned and said, "Yúsuf the constable says that at the gate of Akhsi he met a foot-soldier who told him that the king was in Karmán at such a place; that, without telling the news to any one, he had put the man into close custody, . . . and hastened to you at full speed; and that the Begs know nothing of the matter." I asked him, "What think you of this?" He replied, "They are all your servants; there is nothing left for it but to join them. They will undoubtedly make you king again." "But after such wars and quarrels," said I, "how can I trust myself in their power?" I was still speaking, when Yúsuf suddenly presented himself, and falling on his knees before me exclaimed, "Why should I conceal anything from you? Sultán Ahmad Beg knows nothing of the matter; but *Shaikh Báyazíd Beg has got information where you are, and has sent me hither.*"

'On hearing these words I was thrown into a dreadful state of alarm. There is nothing that moves a man more painfully than the near prospect of death. "Tell me the truth," I cried, "if indeed things are about to go with me contrary to my wishes, that I may at least perform the last rites." Yúsuf swore again and again, but I did not heed his oaths. I felt my strength gone. I rose and went to a corner of the garden. I meditated with myself, and said, Should a man live a hundred, nay, a thousand, years, yet at last he[1] must inevitably make up his mind to die.

> Whether thou live a hundred years or a single day, thou must
> Infallibly quit this palace which delights the heart.

'I resigned myself, therefore, to die. There was a stream in the garden, and there I made my ablutions and recited a prayer of two bowings. Then surrendering myself to meditation I was about to ask God for his compassion, when sleep closed my eyes. I saw (in my dream) Khwája Ya'kúb, son of Khwája Yahyá and grandson of his eminence the Khwája 'Obaid-Allah [a famous saint of Samarkand], with a numerous escort mounted on dappled grey horses, come before me and say, "Do not be anxious. The Khwája has sent me to tell you that he will support you, and seat you on the throne of sovereignty; whenever a difficulty occurs to you, remember to beg his help, and he will at once respond to your appeal, and victory and triumph shall straightway lean to your side." I awoke, with easy heart, at the very moment when Yúsuf the constable and his companions were plotting some trick to seize and throttle me. Hearing them discussing it, I said to them, "All you say is very well, but I shall be curious to see which of you dares approach me."

[1] Here the Persian texts break off suddenly: the rest of the adventure is from the Turki original.

'As I spoke, the tramp of a number of horses was heard outside the garden wall. Yúsuf the constable exclaimed, "If we had taken you and brought you to Tambal, our affairs would have prospered much thereby. As it is, he has sent a large troop to seize you; and the noise you hear is the tramp of horses on your track." At this assertion my face fell, and I knew not what to devise.

'At that very moment the horsemen, who had not at first found the gate of the garden, made a breach in its crumbling wall, through which they entered. I saw they were Kutluk Muhammad Barlás and Bábái Pargári, two of my most devoted followers, with ten to fifteen or twenty other persons. When they had come near to my person, they threw themselves off their horses, and bending the knee at a respectful distance, fell at my feet and overwhelmed me with marks of their affection.'

'Amazed at this apparition, I felt that God had just restored me to life. I called to them at once, "Seize Yúsuf the constable and the wretched traitors who are with him, and bring them to me bound hand and foot." Then turning to my rescuers I said, "Whence come you? Who told you what was happening?" Kutluk Muhammad Barlás answered, "After I found myself separated from you in the sudden flight from Akhsi, I reached Andiján at the very moment when the Kháns themselves were making their entry. There I saw in a dream Khwája 'Obaid-Allah, who said, 'Pádishâh Bábar is at this instant in a village called Karmán; fly thither and bring him back with you, for the throne is his of right.' Rejoicing at this dream, I related it to the big Khán and the little Khán. . . . Three days have we been marching, and thanks be to God for bringing about this meeting . . ."

'We mounted without losing an instant, and made for Andiján. I had eaten nothing for two days. Towards noon we had the luck to find a sheep; we dismounted and settled ourselves comfortably to roast it. After satisfying my ravenous hunger, we set off again, and quickening our pace reached Andiján, doing a distance of five days in two nights and a day. There I embraced the two Kháns, my uncles, and related all that had passed since our separation.'

It all reads like a tale of the Thousand and One Nights, and ends exactly in the orthodox manner; but the graphic narrative is plainly true from start to finish. What happened after this wonderful ride we cannot tell. The Memoirs break off suddenly, and are not resumed until June, 1504, nearly a year and a half later. It may be imagined that Bábar's position as a dependant upon his uncles in his own city of Andiján was even less tolerable than his former penury at Táshkend. But his personal losses may well have been forgotten in presence of the disasters which befel his uncle Mahmúd, to whom 'he almost stood in the place of a son.' The two Kháns were utterly unable to withstand the assaults of Shaibáni. About the middle of 1503 the Uzbeg chief advanced with 30,000 men from Samarkand, sacked Táshkend and Uratipa, and finding the Kháns with an army of 15,000 men near Akhsi, where they were treating for the submission of Báyazíd, threw himself upon them almost before they had time to form in order of battle, and utterly routed them.

Both Kháns were taken prisoners, but Shaibáni, who owed his original success to Mahmúd, said with an air of magnanimity, 'With your help and assistance I have won my power: I took you captive, but I do not kill you; I let you go.' The younger Khán was completely broken by his defeat, and in the following year died in the steppes which he ought never to have left. Mahmúd Khán's fate was more melancholy. He could not be happy in the desert, and after five years was induced to return to Farghána: he was met at Khojend by Shaibáni's officers, who killed him and his five sons on the spot [1]. Such was the gratitude of the Uzbeg.

After the fatal battle of Akhsi in 1503, Bábar 'fled to the hills on the south of Farghána,' near Asfará, and remained in hiding. He twice refers to this fresh exile in his Memoirs [2]: 'When Muhammad Shaibáni Khán defeated Sultán Mahmúd Khán and Aláchá [Ahmad] Khán, and took Táshkend and Sháhrukhíya, I spent nearly a year in Súkh and Húshiyár among the hills, in great distress; and it was thence that I set out for Kábul.'

[1] In 1509, *Tarikh-i-Rashidi*, ed. Elias and Ross, 158, 159, 162.
[2] Erskine and Leyden, 4, 395.

CHAPTER VII

KÁBUL

1504–1505

'THEN it came into my mind,' writes Bábar, 'that it would be better to depart out of Farghána, any whither, rather than go on staying thus without a foothold.' The last attempt to recover his kingdom had begun well, but ended in utter failure. The Uzbegs were now masters of the country; they had followed up the defeat of the Kháns by the execution of Tambal, and were about to drive Khusrau Sháh out of Hisár and Kunduz. Mawarannahr was no longer the place for any son of Tímúr. Northern Persia was still in the hands of Sultán Husain, who had throughout treated Bábar's overtures with unnatural coldness. There remained one chance. Ulugh Beg, Bábar's uncle, the King of Kábul, had died in 1501; his young son, 'Abd-ar-Razzák, had been deposed by a revolution; anarchy had followed, and a usurper, Mukím Beg, an Arghún Mongol from Kandahár, had seized the throne. A strong man of the royal blood might perhaps be able to assert the rights of the family. After some hesitation, Bábar resolved to try.

Little as he suspected it, this was the turning-point in his career. Henceforward, instead of forming one of a crowd of struggling princes contending for the fragments of Tímúr's empire between the great rivers, he stands alone, without a rival or competitor, among the impregnable mountain passes of Afghánistán; until finally the youth who had twice taken and lost Samarkand, and had thrice wandered a penniless exile among the shepherds of the hills of his native land, came out of the Afghán passes by the immemorial road of conquest, and founded an empire in India which lasted, in the hands of his descendants, first in glory, and then in dishonour, down to our own days. From Samarkand to Kábul, and from Kábul to Delhi, has been the road of conquest time after time; until at last another road was ploughed upon the seas, and the Afghán gates were barred by a new race from the islands in the west.

He left his native land with intense regret, and for many years he cherished vague hopes of recovering it. Ill as it had served him, the love of his country was strong in his heart, and it is touching to find him reverting long afterwards to the favourite scenes of his boyhood. He was now leaving them for he knew not what. *Nos patriae fines et dulcia linquimus arva.* He had not yet definitely resolved upon going to Kábul. His first plan was to seek refuge with his kinsmen at Herát, but his views changed as he advanced.

'In the month of Muharram [June, 1504] I set out from the neighbourhood of Farghána, intending to go into

Khurásán, and halted at the summer-cots of Ilák, one of the summer pasturages of the province of Hisár. I here entered my twenty-third year, and began to use the razor to my face. The followers who still clave to me, great and small, were more than two hundred and less than three. Most of them were on foot, with brogues on their feet, clubs in their hands, and tattered cloaks over their shoulders. So poor were we that we had only two tents. My own I gave to my mother; and they pitched for me at every halt a felt tent of cross poles, in which I took up my quarters. Though bound for Khurásán, I was not without hopes, in the present state of things, to manage something among the territories and followers of Khusrau Sháh, where I now was. Hardly a day passed without some one joining me with hopeful news of the country and tribes.'

Bábar, in fact, was tampering with the subjects of his peculiar enemy. It has been suggested that he painted Khusrau Sháh in the blackest colours in order to vindicate his own treatment of him; but he owed the treacherous governor no sort of obligation, and Khusrau's conduct to Mahmúd's sons is enough to explain their cousin's detestation. In justice to the great noble, the Memoirs frankly admit that he was 'far famed for his liberal conduct and generosity, and for the humanity which he showed to the meanest of men, though never to me.' Khusrau at least allowed him to travel through his dominions at a time when any tampering with his army was of vital importance in view of Shaibáni's advance. He seems even to have recognized Bábar as the rightful king; and his brother Báki Beg, with all his family, joined the emigrants and voluntarily shared their fortunes. The probability is that Báki and many other followers of Khusrau saw that their old leader's day was over; and that, if they had to fly, it was better to fly in company, and with the countenance of a distinguished prince of the blood. The young leader's personality, no doubt, counted for much: his name was a synonym for valour—

> Famous throughout the world for warlike praise.

Moreover, the Mongols especially had slight scruples about changing colours, and when Shaibáni's horsemen were tramping the road to Kunduz, Khusrau Sháh himself followed the deserters and offered his allegiance. Bábar received him beneath a tree near the river of Andaráb, and confesses to an ungenerous feeling of triumph when he saw the great man making a score of profound obeisances, 'till he was so tired that he almost tumbled on his face.' The fallen noble had not lost all his spirit, however; for when Bábar cruelly condoled with him on the desertion of his soldiers, Khusrau replied with fine contempt, 'Oh, those scamps have left me four times already: they always come back.' He knew the worth of Mongol loyalty to a nicety, and events proved him right. Some agreement was come to at this meeting, and Khusrau departed for Khurásán with his valuables borne on three or four strings of mules and many camels, whilst Bábar turned his face towards Kábul. He had finally decided that no help was to be found at Herát.

He had now, to his own great astonishment, a considerable army, though mixed and disorderly, and he had acquired eight hundred coats of mail from Khusrau. He was accompanied by his brothers, Jahángír and Násir, in spite of the protests of Báki, who quoted the saying of Sa'di:—

> Ten dervishes may lie on one rug,
> But no country is big enough for two kings.

Besides his brothers, he took with him his cousin Khán Mirzá, otherwise Sultán Wais (the surviving son of Mahmúd), whom he had some trouble in restraining when the young prince claimed the blood revenge from Khusrau for the murder of his kin. The ladies of the family, including Bábar's mother, joined him on the march; but of his old comrades in arms he seems to have had few left besides Káṣim Kochin and Dost Beg. Kambar 'Ali indeed had rejoined him, but he could not keep him: 'he was a thoughtless rude talker, and Báki Beg could not put up with his manners.' This is the last we hear of the friend with the 'muddy brain.' Bábar entered upon his new campaign with new tools. His chief adviser (not excepting his brothers) was now Báki, the brother of Khusrau, and his army was made up chiefly of what he calls 'the Ils and Ulúses,' or wandering tribes; the Mongols who had deserted Khusrau; the wild Hazára mountaineers from beyond Panjhír, and a number of Aimáks from Kunduz. Their adhesion was a compliment to his prestige, but a tax upon his provost marshal. The army was unused to discipline, but perfectly familiar with the art of plunder, and we read of a man flogged to death for outraging the country folk.

Ascending the Hindú Kúsh at Ghúrband, Bábar took the pass of Húpiyán, marching all night, and there for the first time the man from the north saw a brilliant star shining in the southern constellations. 'This cannot be Suhail (Canopus)?' he cried. 'But it is Suhail,' they answered; and Báki quoted—

> O Suhail, how far dost thou shine, and where dost thou rise?
> Thine eye brings luck to him whom thou regardest.

The sun was a spear's length above the horizon when they reached the foot of the valley, and there a council of war was held. Bábar's scouts had already had a successful skirmish with some of the Kábul troops, and had made an important capture. Báki, who took the lead in everything, strongly advised an instant attack on the city, and the whole army, in their mail coats, with armour on their horses, formed up for the assault; Bábar commanded the centre, and his brothers the two wings. There was practically no resistance. The invaders galloped up to the Curriers' Gate, dispersed a feeble attempt to stop them, lost a few men in the staked pits, gave a few cuts and thrusts, and then Kábul surrendered. The usurper Mukím and his family, for whose safety Bábar was concerned, were got away with difficulty; they were mobbed by the disorderly troopers, and the officers could do nothing till the King himself rode up and restored order by the simple method of shooting some of the rioters and cutting down a few others.

Thus, at the beginning of October, 1504, Bábar entered upon his new kingdom at Kábul, 'in the midst of the inhabited part of the world.' He describes it in minute detail, and soon grew to be very fond of his adopted country, and especially of the great garden, the Chár-bágh, which he laid out. Here, as afterwards at Agra, his first thought is for a garden, and no one more honestly believed that—

> God made the garden,—and the city, Cain.

The Kábul kingdom of his day did not comprise what we now call Afghánistán, a term which he limits to the country occupied by Afghán tribes. Kábul itself, with the country round about, was inhabited chiefly by Persian Tájiks, and his sway did not at first extend much beyond Adínápúr in the Khaibar, nor very far south: 'it is a narrow country, but stretching some distance,' he says. The climate and situation of the citadel delighted him, with its cool northern breezes, and the spacious view over meadows and lake:—

> Drink wine in Kábul keep, and send the cup ceaselessly round;
> For Kábul is mountain and sea, city and desert, in one.

'From Kábul you may go in a single day to a place where snow never falls; and in two hours you may find a place of perpetual snow.' There were fruits in abundance, almost to satisfy the taste of one who had been brought up on the melons of Akhsi; yet Bábar imported still more, and added the sour cherry and sugar-cane to the number. But the country was far from rich, grain was raised with difficulty, and the whole revenue of Kábul was only about £35,000.

The new King's description of the country is remarkable for its close observation and keen interest in nature. Bábar knows every animal, bird, and flower; he counts thirty-three species of tulips in one place, and can tell where the rarest sort is found; he knows the habits of bird and beast, and when and how they are to be caught; he tells how the birds cannot fly over the Hindú Kúsh passes in stormy weather, and are thus taken in thousands; and he knows how to lasso herons with a horn at the end of a line, and how to make the fish intoxicated and catch them in shoals. He can tell where the best grass for horses grows, and which pastures are free from mosquitoes. One of his favourite spots was the 'Garden of Fidelity,' where orange trees and pomegranates clustered round a lake, and the whole earth was soft with clover—'the very eye of beauty.' Another was the 'Fountain of the Three Friends,' where three kinds of trees grew, planes, oaks, and the flowering *arghwán*: nowhere else in the country were the two last to be found. Bábar walled the fountain round, and made a seat, for 'when the *arghwán* flowers are in bloom, the yellow mingling with the red, I know no place on earth to compare with it.' In his ruder way, he too felt the subtle influence of flowers that prompted—

> Thoughts that do often lie too deep for tears.

He can tell something, too, about the many races who inhabit his new kingdom, and the dozen tongues they spoke; the dwellers in the wastes, the Hazára, a relic of Chingiz Kaán's armies, still speaking the Mongol language; and the Mahmands, the most powerful of the Afghán tribes; the Orakzáis and Yúsufzáis; or again the people of Káfiristán, 'wine-bibbers, who never pray, fear not God or man, and have heathenish habits.' He is not above superstition, and records the legend of the sand-dune where the sound of ghostly drums and tomtoms is said to be heard; but when he is shown a saint's tomb which rocks if one blesses the Prophet, he investigates the phenomenon, and finds it is caused by an ingenious priest on a scaffold overhead. He makes the attendants come down to the floor, and then they may pronounce as many benedictions as they please, but the tomb remains immovable. Imposture always disgusted him, and he often fell foul of astrologers.

A brief survey convinced him that his new possession was 'to be governed by the sword, not the pen,'—and this, although he had just perfected a new style of calligraphy, 'the Bábari hand,'—and he had to use the sword very soon. He began by overestimating the resources of the people, and, having a large army to support, issued orders for contributions of grain which were beyond the power of his subjects to supply. The result was a rebellion among the Hazára, who had already been plundering, and now refused to pay taxes; so 'we beat them,' says Bábar, 'to our heart's content.' He now perceived that to feed his forces he must forage outside, and he already began to think of the riches of Hindústán. The stories of the soldier of Tímúr, told years before by the old woman among the Ailák shepherds, no doubt recurred to his memory, and the resolve to enter India grew more fixed and clear.

His first expedition, however, hardly touched the promised land of his dreams. He had intended, he says, to enter Hindústán, but was diverted from his project by the urgent advice of Báki. Instead, he fetched a circuit round the Afghán country, down the Khaibar, to Kohát, then past Bannu and the turbulent Bangash district to Isakhail; after which, skirting the foot-hills by Desht or Damán, he crossed the Gomal, and reached the Indus. Even in this slight view of the borders of India, he was impressed with the novelty of the scene. 'I beheld,' he says, 'a new world. The grass was different, the trees different, the wild animals of a different sort, the birds of a different plumage, and the tribes of a different kind. I was struck with astonishment.' For a couple of days he marched along the bank of the frontier river, and then turned inland, crossed the Sulaimán range to the great lake called Áb-i-Istáda or 'Standing Water,' occupied Ghazni, and so returned to Kábul.

The expedition lasted about four months, from January to May, 1505, and besides furnishing grain, bullocks, —and occupation,—gave Bábar a clearer knowledge of the people he had to deal with and the difficulties of the country. The whole route had been a perpetual skirmish with the Afgháns, and Bábar was obliged to be exceedingly careful to avoid surprises. He kept his men under arms at night, ready for an attack, and organized regular rounds of the pickets; if a man was not found on the alert at his post, his nose was slit. The result of his caution was that he was never surprised, and every time he encountered the Afgháns, he beat them, on his own showing: they would then come to him as suppliants, 'with grass between their teeth, as who should say, "I am thine ox."' After a victory, he cut off their heads, and made a 'minaret' of them, like his ancestor Tímúr. His route was studded with these human milestones. At other times he would spare their lives, when he thought it good policy.

The difficulties of the country exceeded his expectations. Toiling over the mountains, he had to abandon his state-pavilion for want of carriage; the horses died from exhaustion; the rains flooded the tents knee-deep, and it was a worn-out army that at last emerged at the 'Standing Water.' Bábar, who had cheerfully composed an ode on the way, was overpowered with delight as he surveyed the grand sheet of water, which stretched to the horizon:—

'The water seemed to touch the sky, and the further hills

and mountains appeared inverted, like those in a mirage, and the nearer hills and mountains seemed to hang between earth and heaven. . . . From time to time, between the water and the sky, something ruddy appeared, like the rosy dawn, and then vanished again, and so went on shifting till we came near; and then we discovered that it was due to immense flocks of wild geese [flamingoes, perhaps], not ten or twenty thousand, but simply innumerable and beyond counting. There were not wild geese alone, but endless flocks of every kind of bird settled on the shores of this lake, and the eggs of countless multitudes of fowl were laid in every cranny.'

On his return to Kábul, he found a budget of news. His brother Násir, who ought to have followed him to the Indus, had been tempted, by a rising against the Uzbegs in Badakhshán, to desert his elder and to cross by the Shibertú pass to try his fortune in a kingdom of his own. Shaibáni was then absent in Khuwárizm, and Khusrau Sháh had also seized the opportunity to make an attempt to recover his lost dominions. He had failed and been taken prisoner, and his head was struck off and sent to the Uzbeg chief. The incident touched Bábar nearly, because as soon as Khusrau's advance was known his old followers began to leave Kábul and rejoin their former master, as he had foretold that they would; but as soon as his death was announced, they came back—'the spirit of discontent was quenched, as when water is thrown on fire.' It was necessary, however, to keep the troops busy, and Bábar found them occupation in the temporary conquest of Khilát-i-Ghilzái, the strong fortress between Ghazni and Kandahár. The garrison obediently came out 'with their bows, quivers, and scimitars, hanging from their necks'; but the place was too far from Kábul to be effectively held at a time when every man might be needed any day to repel the threatened advance of the Uzbegs. No one could be found to undertake to defend it, and it was consequently abandoned.

Bábar was now beginning to feel settled in the saddle. He could afford to assert his authority, and he began by dismissing Báki Beg. This brother of Khusrau had undoubtedly been useful at a critical moment, but, like 'Ali Dost in the Andiján days, he had presumed upon his services. He had become the most powerful Beg of the court, a pluralist who drew all the stamp taxes of Kábul, was captain of the guard, constable of Kábul and Penjhír, and even had drums beaten before his house as though he were actually king. In spite of all these favours and privileges, he was neither grateful nor respectful; 'he was mean, sordid, malicious, narrow-minded, envious, and ill-tempered.' Bábar does not spare the epithets when his dislike is aroused. He determined to get rid of this officious person, and as Báki had several times threatened to resign, one day he took him at his word. The astonished minister reminded him that he had promised not to call him to account until he had been guilty of nine offences: Bábar immediately sent him a list of eleven. Báki had to go, and was soon after murdered among the Yúsufzái Afgháns. Bábar's intriguing and dissipated brother Jahángír fled the country soon after: his absence sensibly relieved the court.

Freed from a presumptuous minister and treacherous kinsfolk, Bábar next undertook the reduction of a turbulent tribe. The Hazára were 'up' again, and were again suppressed, with the usual difficulty attending mountain warfare. As Erskine truly says, it would lead to needless and monotonous detail if one followed Bábar in all his expeditions against the various tribes in the hills and wilds. 'The history of them all is nearly the same. He sets out secretly with a strong light force, marches without halting, comes upon the encampment of the tribe unawares, disperses or slays the men, and carries off the women, cattle, and valuables. Sometimes, however, the clans are on their guard, and he meets with a brave resistance; when, after considerable loss to both parties, victory in the end inclines to the side of disciplined valour. It is hardly possible for governments constituted like those of the East, and possessed of no regular standing army, to subdue, and still less thoroughly to settle, the erratic tribes of the mountains and deserts, who always govern themselves most easily and effectually. Bábar in some instances forced them to acknowledge his supremacy, and to a certain degree restrained their inroads and subjected them to tribute; but in general, down to the time when he conquered Delhi, the Afgháns maintained their independence, only sending tribute with more or less punctuality, according as the means of enforcing it were nearer or more remote.' The Hazára remained unsubdued, though often beaten. Indeed, the relations of Bábar with the wild tribes of Afghánistán, and the nature of his guerilla fighting in that difficult country, may readily be understood by any one who has followed the recent history and campaigns in the north-west frontier of India. Except that Bábar had a few firearms, and the tribes had only bows, the conditions of warfare and the national characteristics were much the same then as in 1898.

It must be remembered that he was established in only a small part of Afghánistán, that his army was composed of mixed and far from trustworthy elements, that the tribes around were in frequent revolt, and that there could be no security so long as Shaibáni pursued his victorious career just the other side of the mountains, and might at any moment follow in Bábar's steps. For years after his conquest of Kábul, the exiled king looked back upon his native land, now overrun by the hardy Uzbegs, with deep regret; and although he was already dreaming those grandiose visions of an Indian Empire, which were not to be realized till twenty years later, his chief preoccupation at first was to protect his rear, and if possible get the better of the victorious chief who had robbed him of his birthright. The only possibility of vanquishing Shaibáni lay in a vigorous combination of the surviving fragments of the family of Tímúr. In pursuit of such a union Bábar now journeyed to Herát.

CHAPTER VIII

HERÁT

1506–1507

SHAIBÁNI KHÁN, after finishing the subjugation of the kingdom of Khuwárizm, by the Sea of Aral, returned to the attack of the remnant of the Tímúrid Empire. At the end of 1505, when all the land between the Sir and the Amu, from Aral to Badakhshán, was his, he prepared to conquer Persia, and began by laying siege to the great city of Balkh, the strongest outpost of Khurásán. Sultán Husain at last was thoroughly roused; he took the field, despite his age and infirmities, and summoned all his kinsmen to his side. Now or never must the Uzbeg invasion be met and rolled back. Among the rest, Bábar was called to the war, and none would more heartily join in a campaign against his own deadliest enemy. To defeat Shaibáni was now his dearest wish: it meant revenge for the loss of Samarkand, it might mean Samarkand regained. In June, 1506, he led his troops out of Kábul, and taking the Shibertú and the 'Toothbreak' (*Dendán-shikán*) passes, descended to Kahmard, and thence past the Aimák country, where 'as all the world was in disorder, every one plundering and usurping other folks' property, my people took some booty from the tilled land as well as from the clans; and we imposed a subvention on the Turks and Aimáks.' His brother Jahángír had been intriguing among these people, and Bábar had chosen this route in order to assert his sovereignty and bring his brother, like a whipped cur, to heel.

At the end of October, after a march of eight hundred miles, he met the sons of Sultán Husain; the old man himself had died in the spring, even before the army left Kábul. The princes were encamped with all the troops they could collect on the bank of the river Murgháb. They were a totally new experience to the hardy soldier. Whatever may have been the comparative luxury of Andiján or Samarkand in the days of his infancy, Bábar had never known the soft delights of cultured ease and magnificent idleness. His own life had been a succession of adventures and privations. He now for the first time became acquainted with the luxurious possibilities of a decadent civilization. Herát, then the capital of Khurásán, had been the home of science and the arts during the long reign of the late sovereign, and the natural capacity of the site had been developed to the utmost. Though it possessed but a single stream within the walls, the gardens without were famous for fertility, and for twenty miles on one side, and nearly ten on another, the country round about was a wilderness of lovely orchards and plantations, and expanses of well-tilled fields, surrounding numerous villas and hamlets.

'Herát,' says Khwándamír, 'is the eye—the lamp that illuminates all other cities; Herát is the soul to the world's body; and if Khurásán be the bosom of the earth, Herát is confessedly its heart.' Its mosques and public buildings were the admiration of the Muhammadan world, and in its hundred colleges some of the most learned men of the East had taught. Among the poets and litterati with whom Husain delighted to surround himself were Jámi, the author of *Yúsuf and Zulaikha*, Mírkhwánd and Khwándamír, the historians, 'Ali Shír, who combined brilliant talents as a commander with the name of the best Turki poet of his age, Biáni, poet, critic, calligrapher, and unsurpassed in trilling on the dulcimer; with astrologers, astronomers, philosophers, theologians, rhetoricians, jurisconsults, critics, versifiers, penmen, musicians, portrait painters, innumerable. Bábar devotes many well-filled pages to a list of the eminent men of the court of Herát, and it is far from complete. In this literary metropolis a poet was often the *arbiter elegantiae*, set the fashion in dress among the *jeunesse dorée*, and suggested aesthetic eccentricities of costume not altogether unworthy of the age of Petronius or even the Victorian epoch. 'Ali Ṣhír was not only a fashionable poet, he was the Beau Brummel of his *monde*, and the ''Ali Shír cravat,' and the ''Ali Shír donkey-pad,' were all the rage among the young voluptuaries of the gay city.

Bábar was quite unaccustomed to luxury such as he now witnessed on joining his cousins on the banks of the Murgháb, and afterwards at Herát, whither, jaded with the fatigues of a mock campaign, they all soon repaired. He describes their splendid pavilions, their divans, and carpets, and cushions, their gold and silver goblets, their profusion of rich dishes and varied wines. At first he is rather shocked: 'My forefathers and family,' he says, 'had always sacredly observed the rules of Chingiz. In their parties, their courts, their festivals, and their entertainments, in their sitting down and rising up, they never acted contrary to the institutions of Chingiz.' But he is no bigot, and adds, 'The institutions of Chingiz certainly possessed no divine authority, that a man should be compelled to conform to them; every man who has a good rule of conduct should follow it, and if the father has done what is wrong the son should change it for what is right.'

Yet he did not at once give way to the temptations of Herát. 'At that time,' he notes, 'I drank no wine,' and there was evidently a struggle before he broke his rule. His cousins respected his abstinence, as a good Muslim's obligation, though too hard a doctrine for weaker brethren like themselves. 'The entertainment,' we read on one occasion, 'was wonderfully elegant. On their trays was every kind of delicacy—kebábs of fowl and goose, and dishes in short of every kind. Badí'-az-zamán's[1] entertainments

[1] Badí'-az-zamán was the eldest son of the late Sultán Husain, but Muzaffar was his favourite son by his best-beloved concubine, Khadija Begum. The two had been chosen joint-heirs, and the dual monarchy ruined the government.

were highly renowned, and this party was certainly free, easy, and unconstrained. During the time I remained on the banks of the Murgháb, I was present twice or thrice at the Mirzá's drinking parties; when it was known that I drank no wine, they did not trouble me by pressing.' Then he began to argue with himself thus—but we will quote the whole passage, as it is admirably illustrative of the society of the time:—

'A few days after, I had an invitation from Muzaffar Mirzá[1], who lived at the White Garden. Khadíja Begum, when dinner was removed, carried him and me to a palace called Terebkhána [or House of Delight] which Bábar Mirzá [the elder] had built. It stands in the midst of a garden, and though small and of only two stories it is a delightful little house. The upper storey is the more elaborate: it has four rooms, one in each corner, enclosing a central large hall; and the four rooms have four royal balconies. Every part of the hall is covered with paintings, . . . executed by order of Sultán Abú-Sa'íd Mirzá, to represent his wars.

'There was a drinking party in the Terebkhána. In the north end of the north balcony two carpets were set facing each other; on one of them sat Muzaffar Mirzá and I, and on the other Sultán Mas'úd Mirzá and Jahángír. As we were guests in Muzaffar's house, the Mirzá placed me above himself, and having filled up a glass of welcome, the cup-bearers began to supply all who were of the party with pure wine, which they quaffed as if it had been the water of life. The party waxed warm, and the spirit mounted up to their heads. They took a fancy to make me drink, too, and bring me into the same ring as themselves. Up to then

[1] See note on previous page.

I had never been guilty of drinking wine, and was therefore practically ignorant of the sensations it produced; yet I had a strong lurking inclination to roam in this desert, and my heart was very fain to cross the stream. In my boyhood I had no wish for it, and knew not its joys or pains. Whenever my father invited me to drink wine, I excused myself and abstained; and after his death, by the protecting care of Khwája Kázi, I continued pure and undefiled: I abstained even from forbidden foods, so was it likely I should indulge in wine? Afterwards, by youthful fancy and natural impulse, I began to hanker for wine, but there was no one about me to help me to gratify my desire; not a soul even suspected my secret longing. . . .

'At this party, among the musicians was Háfiz Háji; Jalál-ad-dín Mahmúd, the flute-player, was there too, and the younger brother of Ghulám Shádi, Shádi Becheh, who played the harp. Háfiz Háji sang well. The people of Herát sing in a low, delicate, *legato* style. There was a singer of Jahángír Mirzá's present, Mír Ján by name, a man from Samarkand, who always sang in a loud, harsh voice, and out of tune. Jahángír, who was far gone, suggested that he should sing, and sing he did, in a horribly loud, rasping, unpleasant tone. The men of Khurásán pique themselves on their good breeding, but many turned their ears away, some frowned, but out of respect for the Mirzá no one ventured to stop him. After the hour of evening prayers we went from the Terebkhána to the new Winter Palace which Muzaffar Mirzá had built. By the time we got there Yúsuf 'Ali Kukildásh, being very drunk, rose and danced; he was a musical man and danced well. Now the party grew very merry and friendly; Jánik sang a Turki song; Muzaffar's slaves performed some lewd, scurvy tricks while the company were hot with wine; the party was kept up late, and did not separate till an untimely hour.'

It seems probable that Bábar did not have his wish after all to drink wine at Herát. His chief adviser, Kásim Beg Kochin, remonstrated so severely with the princes upon their reprehensible design of making their young cousin break his religious habit, that when the next entertainment came off at the eldest prince's, we hear nothing of Bábar's intended initiation in drinking—though unfortunately he had more than enough of it later on—but only of his lack of science as a carver. He could not carve a goose, like many another man of genius, and was obliged to surrender the problem to his cousin: 'Badí'-az-zamán at once cut up the goose, divided it into small pieces, and set it again before me: he was unequalled in this sort of politeness.'

Unfortunately, carving geese and sending the cup round were not the qualities most needed when Shaibáni was in the field. Bábar soon realized that 'the brave barbarian from the north was not to be vanquished by men like these. Their tents of state, their rich carpets, their gorgeous attire and goblets of silver and gold, without adding to their own means of defence, were an incentive to the rapacity of the enemy.' 'The Mirzás,' says Bábar, 'although very accomplished at the social board, or in the arrangements for a party of pleasure, and although they had a charming talent for conversation and society, possessed no knowledge whatever of the conduct of a campaign or of warlike operations, and were perfect strangers to the preparations for a battle, and the dangers and spirit of a soldier's life.' No help was to be expected from these polished gentlemen in withstanding the Uzbeg attack; and now that winter was come, and there could be no campaigning till the next season, Bábar resolved to go home and see what mischief the Turks, Mongols, Aimáks, Afgháns, Hazára, and all the Ils and Ulúses, clans and tribes of various nations and languages, not to mention his own blood relations, had been doing all this while in his new kingdom of Kábul.

At the entreaty of his cousins, the Mirzás, he had spent twenty days in Herát—for 'in the whole habitable world there is not such another city'—he had enjoyed life as he had never enjoyed it before; the youngest of his fair cousins, Ma'súma, had fallen violently in love with him, and they were engaged: but winter was advanced, and on December 24, 1506, he began his return march to Kábul. By the advice of Kásim Beg Kochin he took the mountain road. Bábar had a very high opinion of Kásim, who had been his father's major domo, and in time to come would be governor of his son Humáyún. He describes him as a brave man, a fine sword, and matchless in a foray. It is true, when Bábar's fortunes were overcast, Kásim took service with Khusrau Sháh, but when this great Amír fled before Shaibáni, and his Begs deserted to Bábar, Kásim also returned to his fealty, and his young master welcomed him with affection. In the fight with the Hazára in the glen of Khísh, Kásim had shown prodigious valour, despite his years. 'He was a pious, devout, faithful Muslim,' says Bábar, 'and carefully abstained from all questionable food. His judgement and talents were remarkably good. He was a humorous fellow, and though he could neither read nor write, he had an ingenious and elegant wit.'

Kásim and his master needed all their courage in the adventure that now lay before them. They marched by a route much further south than that they had traversed coming out. It snowed incessantly, and in places the snow rose above the stirrups. They lost their way, their guide became hopelessly puzzled, and never succeeded in finding the road again. They sent out exploring parties, in the hope of lighting upon some stray mountaineers who might be wintering near by, but the scouts came back after three or four days, and reported that no one could be found: the country was absolutely empty of human beings. During the next few days the little army suffered terrible hardships—'such suffering and hardship, indeed,' says Bábar, 'as I have scarcely endured at any other time of my life'; and he forthwith sat down and wrote a poem about it, but it was like to be the last poem he should ever write.

'For about a week we went on trampling down the snow, yet only able to make two or three miles. I helped in trampling the snow; with ten or fifteen of my household, and with Kásim Beg and his sons and a few servants, we all dismounted and laboured at beating down the snow. Each step we sank to the waist or the breast, but still we went on trampling it down. After a few paces a man became exhausted, and another took his place. Then the men who were treading it down dragged forward a horse without a rider; the horse sank to the stirrups and girths, and after advancing ten or fifteen paces, was worn out and replaced by another; and thus from ten to twenty of us trod down the snow and brought our horses on, whilst the rest—even our best men, many of them Begs—rode along the road thus beaten down for them, hanging their heads. It was no time for worrying them or using authority: if a man has pluck and emulation he will press forward to such work of his own accord. . . . In three or four days we reached a cave called Khawál Koti, at the foot of the Zirrín pass [Zard Sang, over the Koh-i-Baba]. That day the storm was terrible, and the snow fell so heavily that we all expected to die together. When we reached the cave the storm was at its worst. We halted at the mouth: the snow was deep, and the path so narrow that we could only pass in single file. The horses moved with difficulty over the beaten, trampled snow, and the days were at the shortest. The troops began to arrive at the cave while it was yet light; when it was dark they stopped; each man had to dismount and halt where he was; many waited for morning in their saddles.

'The cave seemed small. I took a hoe, and scraping and clearing the snow away made a resting-place for myself as big as a prayer carpet near the mouth of the cave; I dug down, breast deep, but did not reach the ground. In this hole I sat down for shelter from the gale. They begged me to go inside, but I would not. I felt that for me to be in warm shelter and comfort whilst my men were out in the snow and drift—for me to be sleeping at ease inside whilst my men were in misery and distress, was not to do my duty by them, or to share in their sufferings as they deserved that

I should. Whatever their hardships and difficulties, whatever they had to undergo, it was right that I should share it with them. There is a Persian proverb that "In the company of friends death is a feast." So I remained sitting in the drift, in the hole that I had dug out for myself, till bedtime prayers, when the snow fell so fast that, as I had been all the time sitting crouched on my feet, I found four inches of snow on my head, lips, and ears: that night I caught cold in the ear. Just then a party that had explored the cave brought word that it was very capacious, and could hold all our people. As soon as I heard this I shook off the snow from my head and face, and went into the cave, and sent to call those who were at hand. A comfortable place was found for fifty or sixty; those who had any eatables, stewed meat, preserved flesh, or anything ready, brought them out; and so we escaped from the terrible cold and snow and drift into a wonderful safe, warm, cozy place, and refreshed ourselves.'

It was by such acts of comradeship and unselfish endurance, at the risk of his life, that Bábar endeared himself to his soldiers. They knew that he took a real personal interest in each one of them, and that every gallant deed or feat of uncomplaining patience was sure to be observed and remembered, whilst in their illness or sufferings they could count on his sympathy and help. He possessed many of the finest qualities of a commander; he knew when to be gentle as well as when to be firm; and above all he never asked his men to do what he would not do himself. Whatever they suffered, he would suffer too. This comradeship with his soldiers accounts for much of Bábar's success, and explains the devotion of the rank and file which enabled him again and again to snatch victory in the most unfavourable conditions.

Fortunately the terrible march was nearly at an end. When they looked forth from the cave the next morning, the storm was over, the snow had stopped, and though the cold was still intense, and many lost their hands or feet from frost-bite, they managed to climb the pass, and the following day the inhabitants of a village down below were amazed to see a weary body of armed men limping down from the snow-clad heights, which the oldest native had never seen crossed by human beings at such a season. The depth of the snow indeed had saved them, and it was only afterwards that they understood how the heavy drifts, through which they had struggled with so much toil, had levelled and softened many a rift and precipice which they could never have passed but for the friendly covering. As they listened to the hidden perils they had escaped, they learnt to be thankful, seated round the fires of the hospitable villagers, taking their fill of good bread and fat sheep, and warmth and sleep, after the hardships of that fearful journey.

As Bábar drew near to Kábul, he learnt that his return had been timed not a moment too soon. A rumour had been spread about that he had been made prisoner in Khurásán, and some of the Mongols who had stayed behind had set up a new king. This was Khán Mirza, the only surviving son of Sultán Mahmúd of Samarkand. Khán Mirza was doubly a cousin, for his father was brother of Bábar's father, and his mother[1] was half-sister of Bábar's mother. It happened that several sympathetic relations of Khán Mirza were at that time in Kábul, including a very strong-minded old woman, Sháh Begum, the Mirza's own grandmother, but only step-grandmother to Bábar, whose own mother and grandmother, his once zealous advocates, were unfortunately dead. There was also an uncle-in-law, Muhammad Husain Mirza Dughlát (father of Mirza Haidar, the author of the celebrated history), who had married Bábar's mother's sister (now dead), and to whom, on going away to Khurásán, the nephew naturally confided a considerable share in the conduct of affairs. There seems to be no doubt that he betrayed his trust, and even his own son's account in the *Tarikh-i-Rashídi* convicts him first of neglect or secret sympathy, and finally of open treason.

The rebels had been laying siege for twenty-four days to the castle of Kábul, which was valiantly defended by some loyal servants of the absent king, when suddenly Bábar burst in upon them. The traitors instantly broke and fled, only to be captured by the loyalists and brought before their injured

[1] This lady, Sultán Nigár Khánim, daughter of Yúnus Khán by Sháh Begum, had no less than four husbands in succession. Firsf she married Mahmúd Mirza, and had the son called Wais, generally known as Khán Mirza. After Mahmúd's death, she became the wife of Uzbeg Sultán of the Kazáks, by whom she had twe daughters; and when Uzbeg died, she wedded Kásim Khán of the Kazáks, and finally Sultán Sa'id Khán of Káshghar.

master. What followed is best told in the words of the chief traitor's son, who sets the conduct of Bábar in a noble and generous light:—

'The Emperor,' he says, 'in conformity with his affectionate nature, without ceremony, and without a sign of bitterness—nay, with the utmost cheerfulness and good humour—came into the presence of his step-grandmother, who had withdrawn her affection from him and set up her grandson as king in his stead. Sháh Begum was confounded and abashed, and knew not what to say. The Emperor, going down on his knees, embraced her with great affection, and said, "What right has one child to be vexed because the motherly bounty descends upon another? The mother's authority over her children is in all respects absolute." He added, "I have not slept all night, and have made a long journey." So saying, he laid his head on Shah Begum's breast and tried to sleep; he acted thus in order to reassure the Begum. He had scarcely fallen asleep when his maternal aunt, Mihr Nigár Khánim [daughter of Yúnus, and widow of Sultán Ahmad, and herself apparently in the plot], entered. The Emperor leapt up and embraced his beloved aunt with every manifestation of affection. The Khánim said to him, "Your children, wives, and household are longing to see you. I give thanks that I have been permitted to behold you once again. Rise up and go to your family in the castle. I, too, am going thither."

'So he went to the castle, and on his arrival all the Amírs and people began to thank God for His mercy. They made the dust of the feet of that loving king *kohl* for their eyes. Then the Khánim conducted Khán Mirza and my father [the treacherous uncle] before the Emperor. As they approached, the Emperor came out to meet them. The Khánim then said, "O soul of your mother! I have also brought the guilty grandson and the unfortunate brother to you. What have you to say to them?" And she pointed to my father. When the Emperor saw my father, he instantly came forward with his wonted courtesy, and smiling openly, embraced him, made many kind enquiries, and showed him marked affection. He then embraced Khán Mirza in like manner, and displayed a hundred proofs of love and good feeling. He conducted the whole ceremony with the utmost gentleness of manner, bearing himself, in all his actions and words, in such a way that not a trace of constraint or artifice was to be seen in them. But, however much the Emperor might try to wear away the rust of shame with the polish of mildness and humanity, he was unable to wipe out the dimness of ignominy which had covered the mirror of their hopes[1].'

As Erskine points out, while this 'clemency was, indeed, founded on strong natural affections, and constitutional strength of feeling,' it was sound policy as well as natural kindness that directed Bábar's conduct in this and many similar acts of mercy. But he felt the treachery of his kindred deeply, especially of the women to whom he had given asylum at his court[2]; whilst as to his uncle, Muhammad Husain, who had so ill requited his trust, he says plainly that had he been cut in pieces he would only have met with his deserts; yet he forgave him for his kinship, and let him depart, only to hear that 'this ungrateful thankless man, this coward, who had been treated by me with such lenity, and whose life I had spared, entirely

[1] *Tarikh-i-Rashidi*, ed. laud., 200–201.

[2] *Memoirs*, E. and L., 217–218.

forgetful of this benefit, abused me and libelled me to Shaibáni,' his new master. Even this did not prevent Bábar's receiving the traitor's son at Kábul with the utmost kindness a few years later.

Such was the end of Bábar's expedition to Khurásán, and of the hopes of repelling Shaibáni. The voluptuous Mirzás of Herát and their beautiful capital soon fell before the brave barbarian from the north, and Bábar was next to be menaced in his own little kingdom, which he had opportunely recovered from the traitors of his own household.

CHAPTER IX

Kábul and Kandahár

1507–1510

Bábar had scarcely returned to Kábul when the news came of the fall of Herát and the extermination of the dynasty of Husain. The King of Kábul was now the only reigning prince of the family of Tímúr, and the dejected adherents of the fallen house rallied round him as their sole hope in the general cataclysm caused by the triumph of Shaibáni. Even the Arghún brothers, Sháh Beg and Mukím, rulers of Kandahár, who boasted a descent from Chingiz, and who had not forgiven Bábar for depriving them of Kábul three years before, turned to him for shelter against the coming storm. The very Mukím, whom he had supplanted in 1504, begged him to come to Kandahár and defend it against the Uzbegs. Bábar took the request as a mark of submission, and with his natural impetuosity marched at once to the rescue. When he arrived before Kandahár, however, he found that he was mistaken[1]. Far from welcoming him as a deliverer and paying homage

[1] This is Bábar's account; the *Tarikh-i-Rashidi* (202) represents the case differently, and states that Bábar sent an envoy to Kandahár to claim Sháh Beg's allegiance to him as the head of the royal house of Tímúr, which was refused.

to him as their king, the Arghún brothers (who had already made terms with Shaibáni) treated him with the cool civility of equals, and even used certain forms in the letters that passed between them which were more customary in addressing an inferior. Bábar was not a meek man, and this insolence was too much for his fiery temper. He immediately prepared for action, and forming up his troops in a meadow near Kandahár, got ready to receive the enemy.

'My whole force,' he says, 'might amount to about two thousand, but . . . when the enemy appeared I had only about a thousand men with me. Though they were few in number, I had been at great pains to train and exercise them to the utmost point. Never, perhaps, were my troops in such perfect discipline. All my personal retainers who were fit were divided into companies of tens and fifties, and I had appointed officers for each, and assigned each company its proper station on the right or the left, so that they were all prepared and fully informed of what they were to do . . . The right and left wings, the right and left [of the centre], the right and left flanks, were to charge on horseback, and were drawn up and instructed to act of themselves without orders from the aides-de-camp; but in general all the troops knew their stations and whom to attack.'

The finer discipline of Bábar's small army told against the greatly superior numbers of the enemy. The account of the battle of Kandahár is too confused to be intelligible, but it appears that after the first rush of the hostile cavalry had driven his vanguard in upon the centre, Bábar's wings pressed steadily on, seized the fords of the rivers, and after a fierce struggle put the Arghún forces to flight. The citadel opened its gates, and the conqueror found himself in possession of amazingly rich treasures: indeed, he declares, in delighted hyperbole, 'no one ever was known to have seen so much money.' It was too much trouble to count it, so it was put into scales and divided by weight. The camp was gorged with plunder and spoils of every description, and the army marched back to Kábul driving asses laden with huge sacks of silver, weighing several hundredweight, which they loaded up as carelessly as if it were forage.

Except for the booty, the expedition was useless. Bábar had hardly been home a week when he learned that his brother Násir, lately returned from Badakhshán, whom he had left at Kandahár with a weak garrison, was shut up in the citadel, and that Shaibáni was vigorously pressing the siege. Luckily a rising in another part of his dominions called the Uzbeg away, and Násir was able to retreat to Ghazni from his untenable position, which was immediately reoccupied by the Arghún brothers. The bare news, however, of Shaibáni's approach had thrown Kábul into consternation. Nothing apparently could check the advance of this terrible Tatar, who had trampled upon all Transoxiana, Khuwárizm, Farghána, and Khurásán, and was now drawing nearer and nearer to the last refuge of the fallen house of Tímúr. To defend Kábul seemed hopeless, and Bábar actually determined to fly. He had experienced Shaibáni's strength before, more than once; the feud was deadly, and probably he never feared any man as he feared the Uzbeg chief. It is the only instance on record of downright panic in the man who ordinarily did not know the meaning of fear. He put a cousin in charge of the city, and gathering his troops together set out for India. He got as far as Adínápúr (now Jalálábád), fighting his way among the Afgháns, and occupied his men in the vain attempt to subdue this truculent people—'robbers and plunderers,' he calls them, 'even in time of peace'—until the news of Shaibáni's retreat emboldened him to return to his capital. The advance into India, which he had so often contemplated, was again postponed.

At this time Bábar assumed a new title,—a name, he says, never before used by any prince of the dynasty of Tímúr: he called himself *Pádisháh*, 'emperor,' and by that style he was ever afterwards known. High-sounding as was the title, and great the wearer's state, he was still far from secure upon his throne. Shaibáni had indeed retreated, and never again troubled his peace, but the difficulties at Kábul were not over. He had left his cousin, 'Abd-ar-Razzák, in command, with his natural want of suspicion, in spite of the fact that this cousin was the son of the late King Ulugh Beg, and had himself sat on the throne of Kábul. The ex-king offered no opposition when Bábar returned to take over the government, but it would have been more than human if he had quite forgotten that he had once worn the crown himself. Had he been strictly loyal to his cousin, the rebellion which followed might not have taken place. Three thousand of the Mongol troops, remnants of Khusrau Sháh's forces, rose in revolt, and proclaimed 'Abd-ar-Razzák king. They were tired of Bábar's just rule, and resented his stern suppression of their innate habits of licence and marauding. The Mongols could not live without the diversions of plunder and rape, and a king who punished these excesses with death was not the sovereign for them. So 'Satan took possession of their brains, and in the place of sound reason substituted vainglory and villainy, the crop of cursed natures.'

The idea of conspiracy and treachery was so utterly foreign to Bábar's open nature, that for a time he refused to believe the rumours that were brought to him of plots and secret meetings, and was taken completely by surprise. At the Iron Gate he was all but captured, and when he reached his camp outside the city he found himself so largely deserted by his men—some to join, others to flee from, the Mongols—that he could only muster five hundred horse. Even the camp bazar was plundered, and many of his trusty followers had hastened into Kábul, not from disaffection, but in the hope of rescuing their families from the horrors of a Mongol orgy. The Memoirs unfortunately break off at this critical moment, and Bábar does not tell us himself of the exciting contest that ensued. We should give him credit for his usual courage:

> No thought of flight,
> None of retreat, no unbecoming deed
> That argued fear

could be expected of Bábar in such a strait; but fortunately we have the testimony of his cousin Haidar, not only that the Emperor led his little force with his own unswerving pluck against the rebels, but that it was 'one of his greatest fights. After much giving and taking of blows and innumerable hand-to-hand conflicts, he broke and routed the foe. In that action he personally and alone engaged five different champions of the enemy, and with brave strokes and sword-cuts put them all to flight.'

The would-be king, 'Abd-ar-Razzák, fell into the conqueror's hands, 'but was treated with generosity and set at liberty.' There is nothing in Bábar's character more noble than his trustfulness and magnanimity towards his rivals, even after they had grossly deceived him. His brother Jahángír (whose drunken habits had before this brought him to the grave) had plotted against him, but Bábar had treated him at Herát with all the affection and respect which he had justly forfeited. His other brother, Násir, had stirred up many of the tribes to desert their sovereign, and had marched with them to Badakhshán in open rebellion, eager to found a separate kingdom; and when he returned, broken and defeated, 'ashamed and distressed at his former doings,' his forgiving brother 'showed him not the least sign of displeasure, but . . . conversed with him, and showed him marks of regard, to dissipate his uneasiness and embarrassment.' He even trusted him with the command of Kandahár, and, when that was lost, with Ghazni. In the same large-hearted way he forgave his cousin ʿAbd-ar-Razzák. Rancour and bearing malice were feelings that Bábar could not understand, at least against his kith and kin: he was sometimes implacable against other scoundrels, though seldom against any one who had ever served him. He would welcome back, over and over again, officers who had deserted him in his hour of misfortune; and, far from bearing ill-will, when Mirza Haidar, son of the Dughlát Amír who had betrayed his trust at Kábul, sought refuge from the vengeance of Shaibáni at his hospitable court, in utter destitution, Bábar gave him a reception which the grateful historian never forgot, though he expresses his sentiments in the turgid manner of a Persian euphuist:—

'When we reached Kábul we were received by Shirun Tagháí, who was maternal uncle to the Emperor and myself, and one of the pillars of state. With a hundred marks of respect he invited me to his house, where I was entertained with distinction and kindness. Later the Emperor sent a message to say that after three days the happy hour would arrive when he would send for me . . . When I came into his presence the joy-diffusing glance of the Emperor fell upon me, and from the excess of his love and the intensity of his kindness, strung pearls and set rubies began to rain down upon me from his benign, jewel-scattering eye. He extended towards me the hand of favour and bade me welcome. Having first knelt down, I advanced towards him. He then clasped me to the bosom of affection, drew me to the breast of fatherly love, and held me thus for a while. When he let me go, he would no longer allow me to observe the formalities of respect, but made me sit down at his side. While we were thus seated he said to me with great benevolence:

"Your father and brother and all your relations have been made to drink the wine of martyrdom; but, thank God, you have come back to me again in safety. Do not grieve too much at their loss; for I will take their place, and whatever favour of affection you could have expected from them, that and more will I show you." With such promises and tenderness did he comfort me, so that the bitterness of orphanage and the poison of banishment were driven from my mind . . . How can I ever show sufficient thankfulness? May God reward him with good things.

'Thus I passed a long time in the service of the Emperor, in perfect happiness and freedom from care; and he was for ever, either by promises of kindness or by threats of severity, encouraging me to study. If he ever noticed any little virtue or new acquisition, he would praise it in the highest terms, commend it to everybody, and invite their approbation. All that time the Emperor showed me such affection and kindness as a fond father shows his son and heir. It was a hard day for me when I lost my father, but the bitterness of my desolation became scarcely perceptible owing to the blessed favours of the Emperor. From this time to the year 918 [1508 to 1512], I remained in his service. Whenever he rode out I had the honour of riding at his side, and when he received friends I was sure to be among the invited. In fact, he never let me be separated from him. When I was studying, for example, directly my lesson was over he would send some one to fetch me. And in this fatherly way did he continue to treat me till the end of my stay[1].'

The grateful recollections of this child, who lived with Bábar from his eighth to his twelfth year, bear the stamp of truth and genuine feeling. There was another refugee at Kábul, who arrived a couple of weeks

[1] *Tarikh-i-Rashidi*, 228–230.

before Mirza Haidar, and who enjoyed almost equal kindness at the Emperor's hands. This was Sa'íd Khán, son of Ahmad Khán, Bábar's Mongolian uncle. He, too, fled from Shaibáni's wrath, and reaching Kábul towards the close of 1508, was at once welcomed with every mark of honour. He used to say in after years: 'Those days that I spent in Kábul were the freest from care or sorrow of any that I have ever experienced, or ever shall experience. I spent two years and a half at the court of this excellent prince, in a continual succession of enjoyments, and in the most complete abandonment to pleasure and absence of preoccupation. I was on friendly terms with all, and made welcome by all. I never suffered even a headache, unless from the effects of wine; and never felt distressed or sad, except on account of the ringlets of some beloved one.' 'There existed,' adds Haidar, 'between these two great princes, perfect accord and love and trust[1].' Sa'íd Khán possessed high rank and great influence, and, as events proved, might become a powerful rival; but there was no trace of jealousy or suspicion in the Emperor's treatment of his guest. He was indeed a perfect host and an incomparable friend.

Two or three years passed by: tranquillity reigned undisturbed at Kábul, whilst wars shook Persia and the Oxus regions almost to ruin. The cousin, Khán Mirza, who like others had once usurped Bábar's throne and been deposed and forgiven, took himself off to found a viceroyalty in Badakhshán, and, doubt-

[1] *Tarikh-i-Rashidi*, 226.

less to their host's relief, carried with him the intriguing grandmother Sháh Begum, who came of the ancient stock of the Badakhshán kings, who traced their descent, they said, from Alexander the Great. Sháh Begum went even further: 'It has been our hereditary kingdom,' she declared, 'for 3,000 years. Though I, being a woman, cannot myself attain to the sovereignty, yet my grandson, Khán Mirza, can hold it. Males descended from me and my children will certainly not be rejected.' Nor were they, for Khán Mirza reigned in Badakhshán till his death, in faithful subjection to his cousin.

Relieved of the presence of possible conspirators, the Emperor divided his time between the inevitable 'punitive expeditions' against the Afghán tribes, the delights of great hunting parties, and the pleasure he always took in beautifying his capital and laying out gardens and parks. The continual round of enjoyments described by his visitor was no doubt shared to the full by the Emperor, the centre and life of his society; but the break in the Memoirs from 1508 to 1519 deprives one of the minute record of the daily occupations of the writer which is so full and interesting at other periods, and one is thrown back upon the imagination to fill in the picture from the analogy of earlier and later years.

CHAPTER X

SAMARKAND ONCE MORE

1510–1514

IN the midst of this uneventful interval, Bábar was suddenly called to action. A messenger arrived at Kábul in the winter of 1510 with a letter from Khán Mirza. It related how Sháh Ismá'íl, the new ruler of Persia, founder of the imperial Safavi line of Sháhs, had fought and conquered Shaibáni Khán, and how the Uzbegs were flying from Khurásán over the Amu to Kunduz. The passes were blocked with snow, but Bábar heeded it not. He was once more inspired with the dream of his life, the dream of empire on Tímúr's throne; mere obstacles of ice and snow were nothing to one spurred on by

> Ambition, the desire of active souls,
> That pushes them beyond the bounds of nature
> And elevates the Hero to the Gods.

The recovery of a lost Eden was before his eyes, and he set off at once to join forces with the Persians, and give the final blow that should crush the great oppressor of his house. He did not then know that after the fatal battle near Merv, Shaibáni was smothered among a heap of dying men and horses, and his head was presented to Sháh Ismá'íl, who had the skull set in gold for a drinking cup. In spite of this calamity, the Uzbegs had no thought of evading a battle with Bábar, whatever they might have done had the Sháh himself been at the front. Hamza Sultán, one of their chiefs, marched to meet him, but the two armies missed each other on the way, and each arrived at the other's camping-ground only to find it deserted. It was a game of cross-purposes, and each suspecting some insidious ruse on the part of the other, and being totally misinformed as to their respective strengths, beat a hasty retreat, thanking God for a merciful escape.

The Uzbeg power was still very strong in Transoxiana; though Shaibáni was dead, his veteran captains still led the tribes; and Bábar could not venture to attack them until he was reinforced by a body of Turkmán troops sent to his support by the Persian Sháh. The enemy, still greatly superior in numbers, courted the issue of battle, and Bábar withdrew at his top speed to a strong position in the mountain passes towards Abdara, where he awaited their attack. The battle took place early in 1511. 'At midnight news came that the Uzbegs were advancing in full force; the commanders announced this simultaneously to the whole army, and up to daybreak every man was busy getting his arms ready. About sunrise our pickets came in and reported that the Uzbeg army was approaching. Thereupon the Emperor mounted his horse and rode to the top of some rising ground.'

> And from their tents the Tartar horsemen filed
> Into the open plain.

The enemy were deploying on the plain, and the only road by which they could approach was in a ravine between two hills. They preferred to climb one of the hills, rather than risk being shut up in the gorge. One of their chiefs led 10,000 men to the assault. Khán Mirza was given the post of honour, and he hurried to meet the climbing squadrons. The furious charge of the Uzbeg horse bore down every one before it, and they had almost reached the Mirza himself, when an opportune reinforcement saved the day.

It was the boy Haidar who was thus proudly able to reward his benefactor. Bábar had brought him most reluctantly from Kábul, only at his piteous entreaty not to be left behind; on the way a number of Haidar's hereditary retainers had joined him, and these veterans Bábar had hurriedly dispatched to the rescue of Khán Mirza. Haidar himself he kept at his side—'you are still too young for such business' he said—and one can imagine the eager joy of the young prince as he watched beside his patron and saw his men, his very own followers, rallying the Emperor's vanguard, and driving the enemy down the hill. It was a glorious moment for him, and when one of his own people brought the first prisoner to the Emperor, and Bábar said, 'Inscribe the name of Mirza Haidar upon the first trophy,' he was radiantly happy.

The battle raged all day on the left wing; but when it grew dusk, and the enemy began to fall back, in order to pitch a camp near water, Bábar's men seized the moment of confusion, and rushed down in hot pursuit, shouting *Hai! Hai!* at the top of their voices, and charging with reckless fury on the retiring squadrons. The result was a total rout; the generals were captured and killed, and for a whole day the fugitives were hotly pressed.

The end of the Uzbeg domination in Mawarannahr seemed at hand. They abandoned Karshi, they were driven out of Bukhárá, they fled from Samarkand into the deserts of Turkistán. With the consent of his ally the Sháh, Bábar once more mounted the throne of Samarkand, which he had twice before filled. 'All the inhabitants of the towns of Mawarannahr, high and low, nobles and poor men, grandees and artisans, princes and peasants, alike testified their joy at the advent of the Emperor. He was received by the nobles, while the others were busy with the decoration of the city. The streets and bazars were draped with cloth and gold brocades, and drawings and pictures were hung up on every side. The Emperor entered the city in the middle of the month of Rejeb in the year 917 [October, 1511] in the midst of such pomp and splendour as no one has ever seen or heard of before or since.'[1] Never before had his dominions stretched so wide and far. From Táshkend and Sairam on the borders of the deserts of Tartary,

[1] *Tarikh-i-Rashidi*, 246.

to Kábul and Ghazni near the Indian frontier, in Samarkand, Bukhárá, Hisár, Kunduz, and Farghána, Bábar was king. He abandoned all thoughts of India, despised his little Afghán throne, which he presented to his brother Násir; henceforth he resolved to reign in the seat of Tímúr on the imperial throne of Samarkand.

But the triumph was short-lived. The fates had decreed that, try as he might, Bábar should not hold Tímúr's sceptre. The obstacles were not all from without: they were partly of his own making. In the absence of his autobiographical reminiscences of this critical period, it is difficult to determine his exact position and policy, but from the statements of Haidar and Khwándamír, confirmed in a striking manner by a coin in the British Museum, it is evident that he held the throne of Samarkand as the vassal of Sháh Ismá'íl, and that in dress and even in religious doctrine he conformed to the rule of his suzerain [1]. To Bábar, who was an easy-going Muslim, too well read in Persian poetry to be shocked at heresy, the change probably meant very little, but to his subjects it represented the sort of effect that incense and monstrance would produce in an 'Auld Licht' kirk. For the Sháh belonged to the fanatical Shiah sect, abhorred by orthodox Sunnites, whilst the people of Samarkand and Bukhárá were the most bigoted Muslims of the straitest orthodoxy to be found outside

[1] *Tarikh-i-Rashidi*, 246, 259; R. Stuart Poole, *Catalogue of Persian Coins in the British Museum*, xxiv ff.

the Holy City of Medina. When they saw their Emperor and his followers going about in the garb of the 'red-heads' (Kizilbásh), with the symbolical twelve-pointed cap and its long puggaree of red cloth —the badge of schismatics; when they fingered coins bearing the heretical formulas of the Shiah, and setting Sháh Ismá'íl's name in the place of honour above Bábar's; when they heard the orthodox Caliphs cursed from the pulpit, and saw their holy teachers murdered for steadfast non-juring:—their enthusiasm died away, their loyalty cooled, they lampooned their sovereign's strange disguise, and they began almost to regret the cruel tyranny of Shaibáni, who might be a devil but was at least an orthodox fiend.

Bábar soon found that he had lost the support of his subjects, and a defeat at Kul Malik, where an Uzbeg leader with only 3,000 men repulsed the imperial army of 40,000, compelled him finally to abandon a throne which he dared not defend, and to fly, for the third and last time, from the city of his ambition. He left Samarkand in May, 1512, after a reign, or viceroyalty, of only eight months. In vain the Sháh sent him large reinforcements of 60,000 'red-heads' under a savage and relentless general, whose cruelty disgusted his humane ally. Nothing could save him. The Uzbegs were not to be denied. At the last fight (November, 1512) at Ghujduwán or Ghazdiván, taking advantage of every wall and cover, they 'began to pour forth their arrows from every corner, so that very soon the claws of

Islám twisted the hands of heresy and unbelief, and victory declared for the true faith. . . . They sent Mir Najm and all the Turkmán Amírs [of Persia] to hell,'[1] and it cannot be doubted that they deserved their fate.

Bábar fled, 'broken and crest-fallen,' to Hisár. Here the Mongols, turning, as usual, against the weaker side, revolted, attacked his quarters by night, and the Emperor, leaping out of bed, barely managed to escape into the fort. They had made proposals some time before to Sa'íd Khán offering to make away with the Emperor in his favour; but Sa'íd had replied that when he was buffeted in the waves of calamity during the hurricane of Shaibáni's conquests, he had been saved upon the island of Bábar's benevolence, and he could not play so ignoble and ungrateful a part towards his preserver. So rare an example of Mongol gratitude is worth recording; but it did not prevent the revolt of the treacherous tribesmen, who now laid waste the whole province of Hisár, and squandered its wealth and crops and cattle. A terrible famine was the result of their devastating violence, 'the living ate the dead, and then fell upon one another.' A pestilence succeeded, and then winter came on with excessive severity; there was a protracted snowfall, till 'the plains became like hills

[1] *Tarikh-i-Rashidi*, 261. Even Haidar, as an orthodox Muslim, utterly condemns his beloved patron's traffic with heretics, and probably from this date there came a certain coolness between them. They never met again.

and the hills like plains'; and at last the Uzbegs came to finish the work. They fell upon the Mongols, who threw themselves into the river Surkháb: 'most of the wretches passed through the water to the flames of hell; some few escaped; and all those who did not reach the river went to hell by way of the flashing scimitar. Those that survived were taken prisoners, and all the suffering that they had inflicted upon the people in Hisár during a whole year, God Almighty, by the hand of 'Obaid-Allah Khán, now caused to descend upon them in one hour.'

Bábar had watched these calamitous doings from his refuge at Kunduz, whither he had contrived to escape. From the summit of success and wide authority, he was reduced to great distress and even positive want. He had lost his kingdom, and the return of the Uzbegs deprived him even of the chance of recovering the province of Hisár. He might have claimed a suzerain's right, and taken Badakhshán from Khán Mirza; but he was too generous for that. He 'bore the situation patiently, and ... at last despairing altogether of recovering Hisár, he returned to Kábul' in 1513 or 1514[1]. It was perhaps the bitterest experience of his life. He had barely regained the ancestral throne of Tímúr, only to lose the respect of his subjects, to be worsted by the enemy, and to see his beloved country harried and destroyed by the Mongols whom he loathed.

[1] *Tarikh-i-Rashídi*, 260-263.

Deprived of the last hope of recovering his own land, the banished Emperor turned his eyes eastward. Rejected by his countrymen, Bábar might have said with St. Paul, 'Henceforth I turn to the Gentiles.'

CHAPTER XI

The Invasion of India

1519–1524

'From the time when I conquered the land of Kábul in 910 [1504–5] till now,' wrote Bábar in 1526, 'I had always been bent on subduing Hindústán. Sometimes, however, from the misconduct of my Amírs and their dislike of the plan, sometimes from the cabals and opposition of my brothers, I was prevented. . . At length these obstacles were removed; there was no one left, high or low, gentle or simple, who could dare to urge a word against the enterprise. In 925 [1519] I gathered an army, and taking the fort of Bajaur by storm in about an hour, put all the garrison to the sword. Then I advanced into Bhíra, where I prevented all marauding and plunder, imposed a tax upon the inhabitants, and dividing the proceeds among my troops, returned to Kábul. From that time till 932 [1526], I specially devoted myself to the affairs of Hindústán, and in the space of these seven or eight years I entered it five times at the head of an army. The fifth time, God Most High, of His mercy and grace, cast down and defeated so powerful an enemy as Sultán Ibráhím, and made me master and conqueror of the mighty empire of Hindústán.'

So wrote the first Emperor of India after the memorable victory at Pánípat, on the field where the fate of Hindústán has thrice been decided. He was apt to take the impression of the moment for a permanent conviction, and it may be questioned whether he had really set the conquest of India before his eyes ever since his arrival in Kábul. The evidence points to a much stronger attraction towards Samarkand. When that fervent ambition lay dead, killed by repeated failure and the indomitable ascendancy of the Uzbegs, then, and not before, did Bábar's dreams of an Indian empire take distinct form. After that it was five years before he made the first move, and more than twenty years had passed since his conquest of Kábul, before he marched into Delhi. Men of his impetuous and daring nature do not stifle a burning ambition for twenty years, and it was only when a still more ardent hope was quenched that the alternative began to become urgent, and even then the plan took five years maturing.

Those five years must have been spent in organizing his little kingdom, which had been allowed to degenerate under the loose control of his youngest brother. Násir Mirza went out to meet Bábar with all honour, on his return from the ill-fated campaigns beyond the Oxus, and at once resigned the government, retiring to his former command at Ghazni, where drink, the prevailing vice of the Mongols, soon made an end of the weak voluptuary, as it had before of his brother Jahángír. A rebellion of his Mongol Begs followed upon his death, but Bábar was by this time hardened to these periodical outbreaks, defeated the traitors in a pitched battle, and quickly suppressed the revolt. He had more troublesome work to reduce the hill tribes to order, and his success was only partial; but he secured the loyalty of the great clan of the Yúsufzáis by marrying a daughter of one of their chiefs, and he received the submission of the rulers of Swát and Bajaur. At this point (1519) the Memoirs, of which we have been deprived for a dozen important years, recommence (though only in a fragment covering twelve months), and the description of the siege of Bajaur—the prologue to the first act of the invasion of India—presents a vivid picture of the fighting of those days, and is peculiarly interesting for its account of the use of European (Feringi) artillery:—

'On Thursday, 4 Muharram [Jan. 6, 1519], I ordered the troops to put on their armour, to prepare their weapons, and to mount ready for action. The left wing I ordered to proceed higher up than the fort of Bajaur, to cross the river at the ford, and to take their ground to the north of the fort; I ordered the centre not to cross the river, but to station themselves in the broken and high grounds to the north-west; the right wing was directed to halt to the west of the lower gate. When Dost Beg and the officers of the left wing halted after crossing the river, a hundred or a hundred and fifty foot sallied from the fort and assailed them with flights of arrows; but they, for their part, received the attack, returned the volley, chased the enemy back to the fort and drove them under the ramparts. Maula 'Abd-al-Malik of Khost madly pressed on his horse and galloped up to the foot of the wall; and if scaling ladders and siege-shields had been ready we should have been inside the castle that moment . . . The people of Bajaur had never seen matchlocks, and at first were not in the least afraid of them, but, hearing the reports of the shots, stood opposite the guns, mocking and playing unseemly antics. But that day Ustád 'Ali Kúli [the chief gunner] brought down five men with his matchlock, and Wali Khazin killed two, and the other musketeers shot well and bravely, quitting their shields, mail, and "cowheads" [or penthouses], and aiming so truly that before night seven to ten Bajauris were laid low; whereupon the defenders of the fort became so frightened that not a man ventured to show his head for fear of the matchlocks. As it was now evening, orders were given that the troops should be drawn off for the present, but should prepare implements and engines for assaulting the fortress in the morning twilight.

'On Friday, at the first dawn of light, orders were given to sound the kettle-drum for action. The troops all moved forward in the stations assigned to them, and invested the place. The left wing and centre having brought at once an entire *túra* [penthouse] from their trenches, applied the scaling ladders, and began to mount . . . Dost Beg's men reached the foot of a tower on the north-east of the fort, and began undermining and destroying the walls. Ustád 'Ali Kúli was also there, and that day too he managed his matchlock to good purpose; the *Feringi* piece was twice discharged[1]. Wali Khazin also brought down a man with

[1] The Memoirs contain frequent references to the big guns (*feringihá*) of the master cannoneer Ustád 'Ali Kúli. In November, 1526, we read of the casting of one of these. Bábar was present at the operation. 'Around the place where it was to be cast were

his matchlock. On the left of the centre, Malik Kutb 'Ali, having climbed the wall by a scaling-ladder, was for some time engaged hand to hand with the enemy; at the lines of the main body, Muhammad 'Ali Jangjang and his younger brother Nauróz, scaling a ladder, fought bravely with sword and spear; Bábá Yasáwal, going up another ladder, set about demolishing the parapet with his axe. Many of our men climbed boldly up, and plied the enemy with their arrows so that never a head was shown above the works; others, despite all the enemy's exertions and harassments, despising their bows and arrows, busied themselves in breaking

eight furnaces, . . . below each of which was a channel running down to the mould in which the gun was to be cast. On my arrival they opened the holes of all the furnaces; the liquid metal flowed down by each channel, and entered the mould. After some time the flow of metal ceased, before the mould was full. There was some oversight. . . . Ustád 'Ali was in terrible distress, and like to throw himself into the molten metal. Having cheered him up and given him a robe of honour, we succeeded in softening his humiliation. Two days after, when the mould was cool, they opened it. Ustád 'Ali in great delight sent to tell me that the chamber of the gun for the shot was without a flaw, and that it was easy to form the powder chamber.' These guns, therefore, could be made in two pieces. Later on Bábar went to see the gunner 'fire that same great gun of which the ball-chamber had been uninjured at the time of casting, and the powder-chamber of which he had afterwards cast and finished. . . . It was discharged about afternoon prayers, and carried 1600 paces'—a remarkable performance for the time. In November, 1527, 'Ustád 'Ali fired a large ball from a cannon; though the ball went far, the gun burst in pieces.' Eight men were killed. In February, 1528, we find cannon used to protect a pontoon party, and for three or four days Ustád 'Ali contrived to discharge his gun sixteen times a day, which Bábar considered remarkably good. These large cannon, of which there were evidently very few in any of Bábar's battles, were supplemented by casting machines, such as stone-slings and mangonels. (See *Memoirs*, E. and L., 343, 344, 351, 374, 379.)

through the walls and demolishing the defences. It was breakfast time (*chast*) when the tower on the north-east, which Dost Beg's men were undermining, was breached; whereat the enemy were forthwith driven in, and the tower was taken. At this moment the men of the main body, scaling the walls, also entered the fort. By God's favour and grace we took this strong castle in a couple of hours.'

It is a piteous story: the unhappy Bajauris with their bows and arrows could make no stand against the mysterious matchlocks, primitive as they were; and their smoking muzzles and sharp reports, and the heavy boom of the strange 'Feringi' cannon, must have produced a consternation like black magic. The end was still worse: 'As the men of Bajaur were rebels, rebels to the followers of Islám, and as, besides their rebellion and hostility, they followed the customs and usages of the infidels, while even the name of Islám was extirpated among them, they were all put to the sword, and their wives and families made prisoners. Perhaps upwards of 3,000 were killed.' Bábar records the brutal massacre with righteous satisfaction; despite his generosity and nobility of character, the savage Mongol nature peeps out sometimes. He cut off the heads of the chiefs, and sent them to Kábul as trophies of victory; a pyramid of skulls was built near the ill-fated fortress. Bringing in heads was an honourable feat among Bábar's fellows, and we read of the distress of a scout who successfully cut off an Afghán's head, but had the misfortune to mislay it on his way back. Later, in India, when an attempt was made to poison him, the Emperor took a bloody revenge: the taster was cut in pieces, the cook flayed alive, a woman trampled under the elephants, and another woman shot. Cultured in the humanities, Bábar sometimes forgot to be humane.

From Bajaur the Emperor marched east through Bunír, and fording the Indus, on Feb. 17, 1519, above Attok, followed by his infantry on rafts, he pushed on into the Panjáb, intending to occupy Bhíra, which then lay on the west of the Jhílam. 'We were always full of the idea of invading Hindústán,' he says; 'and as Bhíra was upon the borders and near at hand, I conceived that if I were now to push on without baggage, the soldiers might light upon some booty.' He arrived there without opposition; levied a contribution of over £16,000 on the inhabitants, and sternly suppressed all excesses on the part of his soldiers. He claimed the Panjáb as his inheritance in right of Tímúr's conquest and occupation more than a century before—he had been reading the *Zafar Náma* to refresh his memory of his great ancestor's campaigns —and 'as I reckoned the countries that had belonged to the Turks as my own territories, I permitted no plundering or pillage.' Conscious of his right, such as it was, he even sent an ambassador to explain the situation to the King of Delhi, the actual sovereign of the Panjáb, but the envoy was detained at Lahore, and sent back with his mission unfulfilled.

Having secured the submission of Bhíra, Khusháb, 'the country of Chenáb'—probably between the rivers

Jhílam and Chenáb—Bábar appointed governors from among his Begs, and set out for Kábul. He had, so to speak, 'pegged out a claim' in the north of the Panjáb, but he must have been well aware that it was liable to be 'jumped'—as indeed it was, the moment his back was turned. His army of at most 2,000 men was not equal to larger efforts, his horses were done up, and his chief object had been plunder, of which he had no cause to complain. On his way back he passed north of the Salt Range, and after a sharp skirmish with the Gakars, took their capital, Perhála, and received the submission of several tribes. He doubtless reached Kábul by the Kuram pass. The expedition had not been fruitless, though it left no very permanent traces.

A very singular fact appears prominently throughout Bábar's diary of this campaign. In spite of arduous and responsible duties, he confesses, with his unique frankness, that he was frequently intoxicated, and had become indeed a regular, systematic, deliberate drunkard. As we have seen, before his visit to his cousins at Herát he had never tasted wine, and though he was sorely tempted to begin among such jovial boonfellows, the influence of his prime minister seems to have checked him. We hear nothing of his drinking until January of this year, 1519, when we read of his enjoying the wine of Káfiristán at the castle of Bajaur. A few days later he is eating the 'pleasant, but highly inebriating *Kimál*'—apparently a powerful species of tipsy-cake—which affected him so 'strangely' that he could not attend his council. Soon afterwards we find him taking a bolus (*ma'jún*), or in other words eating hemp or hashísh, called in India *bhang*. Late in life he took opium, which made him very sick; but as a rule arack, wine, and *bhang* served his purpose—anything but beer, which he could not stomach.

There is no telling when he began these habits, but by 1519 he was a steady toper. The least thing serves him as an excuse. He sees a lovely view—and has a drinking party; or 'the crops were uncommonly fine'—another bout; 'I had an early cup by Kábil's tomb'; at noon-day prayers[1]—a drinking party; after evening prayers—a drinking party; a tribute offering arrives—he takes his *bhang* lozenge; he cuts his hair—a bout ensues; the Bágh-i-Wafá was such a beautiful spot that 'we drank a quantity of wine, and took our regular morning cup: when I had no drinking parties I had parties for *bhang*.' Sailing on a raft, he 'drank all the way.' His friends would gather round him under the Tál trees, among the orange groves, or beside a canal; the musicians played, and they drank till they were merry. It was a rule that every man who sang a Persian song—one of Bábar's own composition, sometimes—should have his glass, and every one who sang a Turki song, another; but on rare occasions it was enacted that if

[1] The frequent reference to prayers in connexion with his drinking bouts does not imply any profanity. The stated hours of prayer form the usual divisions of the Muhammadan day, like the primes and nones of Europe.

a man became drunk, he must be removed, and another take his place.

As every one knows, when Orientals drink at all, they generally do it, not for the bouquet, or for gentle exhilaration, but for the express purpose of getting drunk. This was Bábar's case. In the course of the return march from the Panjáb we read: 'About the time of noon-day prayers, I mounted to take a ride, and afterwards going on board a boat, we had a drinking bout. . . We continued drinking spirits in the boat till bed-time prayers, when, being utterly drunk, we mounted, and, taking torches in our hands, came at full gallop back to the camp from the river-side, falling sometimes on one side of the horse, and sometimes on the other. I was miserably drunk, and next morning, when they told me of our having galloped into camp with lighted torches in our hands, I had not the slightest recollection of it.' The Memoirs are full of the oddest bacchanalian scenes; for example:—

'Towards the bow of the vessel a space was roofed in. It had a level platform above, and I and some others sat on the top of it. A few others sat below the scaffolding. Towards the stern of the ship, too, there was a place for sitting: Muhammadi, with Gedai and Na'man, sat there. We continued drinking spirits till after noon-prayers. Disliking the spirits, we then took to *bhang*. Those who were at the other end of the vessel did not know that we were taking *bhang*, and continued to drink spirits. About night prayers we left the vessel, and mounting our horses returned late to camp. Muhammadi and Gedai, thinking that I had been taking nothing but spirits, and imagining that they were doing an acceptable service, brought me a pitcher of liquor, carrying it by turns on their horses. They were extremely drunk and jovial when they brought it in. "Here it is," they said; "dark as the night is, we have brought a pitcher. We carried it by turns." They were informed that we had been using a different thing. The *bhang*-takers and spirit-drinkers, as they have different tastes, are very apt to take offence with each other. I said, "Don't spoil the cordiality of the party; whoever wishes to drink spirits, let him drink spirits; and let him that prefers *bhang* take *bhang*; and let not the one party give any idle or provoking language to the other." Some sat down to spirits, some to *bhang*. The party went on for some time tolerably well. Bábá Ján, the player on the kabúz, had not been in the boat; we had sent for him when we reached the royal tents. He chose to drink spirits. As the spirit-drinkers and *bhang*-takers never can agree in one party, the spirit-bibbers began to indulge in foolish and idle talk, and to make provoking remarks on *bhang* and *bhang*-takers. Bábá Ján, too, getting drunk, talked very absurdly. The tipplers filling up glass after glass for Tardi Muhammad, made him drink them off, so that in a very short time he was mad drunk. Whatever exertions I could make to preserve peace were all unavailing; there was much uproar and wrangling. The party became quite burdensome and unpleasant, and soon broke up.'

It was worse on November 1–2, when they began drinking in the Emperor's tent in the morning, kept at it till night, and the following morning took the customary cup, and 'getting intoxicated, went to sleep.'

'About noon-day prayers we left Istálíf, and I took a bolus (of *bhang*) on the road. . . . While I was riding round the harvest fields, such of my companions as were fond of wine began to contrive another drinking bout. Although I had taken *bhang*, yet as the crops were uncommonly fine, we sat down under some trees that had yielded a plentiful load of fruit, and began to drink. We kept it up there till bed-time prayers.'

Ten days later we find an extraordinary picture of the Emperor's pleasures. They had left the Chárbágh Palace about noon, and dismissing their servants, arrived late, 'about the time of the first sleep,' at their friend Tardi Beg's underground conduit, whence that choice spirit—who, by the way, began life as a dervish, and ended as a distinguished general—hastened forth to greet them.

'I well knew,' writes Bábar, 'Tardi Beg's thoughtless, profuse turn, and that he did not dislike his glass. I had brought about four guineas with me, and gave them to him to get wine and everything ready for an entertainment, as I wished to make merry with some jolly companions. He set out for Behzádi to fetch wine, and I sent my horse by one of his servants to graze in the valley while I sat near the water-course on a rising ground. It was past nine when Tardi Beg came back with a pitcher of wine, and we set about drinking it. While he was fetching it Muhammad Kásim Barlás and Sháhzáda, who had guessed what he was after but did not suspect that I was in the affair, dogged him on foot: so we invited them to join the party. Tardi Beg said that Húlhúlanka wished to drink with us, and I said, "I have never seen a woman drink wine: call her in." He also sent for a kalandar [dervish], called Sháhi, and a man belonging to the water-works, who played the rebeck. We sat drinking wine on the hill behind the water-run till evening prayers; then we went to Tardi Beg's house, and drank by candlelight till after bed-time prayers. It was a wonderfully amusing and guileless party.'

Yet Bábar was up and mounted at the roll of the kettle-drum, and reached his first halt before sunrise. He must have possessed an amazing constitution to survive this treatment. After two more nights of revelry we find him standing in rapt contemplation before an apple-tree, admiring the exquisite colours of the autumn leaves, 'which no painter, however skilful, could depict.' He is always curiously observant of the beauties of nature; he delights in the discovery of spikenard, which he had not found before; and he is never weary of expatiating on the loveliness of the flowers in his favourite gardens. Dissipation never dulled his appreciation of such delights, or his pleasure in poetry and music:—

> A Book of Verses underneath the Bough,
> A Jug of Wine, a Loaf of Bread—and Thou
> Beside me singing in the Wilderness!
> Oh! Wilderness were Paradise enow!

Nor did he lose his nerve, for in the midst of this debauchery he joins vigorously in hunting 'the arm'd rhinoceros and th' Hyrcanian tiger.' He does not seem in the least ashamed of his excesses—on the contrary he often winds up a tale of unconscionable revelry with the words, 'It was a rare party,' or, as above, 'a wonderfully amusing and guileless party.' Evidently he agreed that—

> Man, being reasonable, must get drunk;
> The best of life is but intoxication.

When he had fever, indeed, he was forced to abstain, but even then nothing would satisfy him but his friends must come and drink in his room, so that he might study the effects of wine upon different temperaments from the critical point of view of strict sobriety.

He was, however, fastidious in deportment, even in drinking, and required that his friends, however drunk they might be, should 'carry their liquor like gentlemen.' When they grew uproarious with 'the turbulent mirth of wine,' or foul-mouthed, or idiotic, he was disgusted. Reprobate as he was in this respect, he had his code of morals. He never pressed a man to drink who did not wish it, and he refused to hold a bout in a private house when his host, a kázi, protested that such a thing as wine had never been seen there. Clearly he was a man of scruples—on occasion. Moreover he appears to have been always able to resist temptation when work was to the fore. We never hear of his being in the slightest degree overcome or incapable when his army needed his command, or the enemy were at hand; and we may be sure that if it had happened he would have told us with the utmost candour. He could never have waged his later wars in India unless he had held himself in hand, and accordingly we hear little of drinking parties when once he was on the campaign.

He seems, indeed, to have entered upon his course of regular intemperance with a deliberate intention of carrying it on for a definite period. 'As I intended,' he says in 1519, 'to abstain from wine at the age of forty, and as I now wanted somewhat less than a year of that age, I drank wine most copiously.' Undoubtedly he made the most of the interval, but unhappily he did not stick to his word. There is another gap in the Memoirs from 1520 to 1525, but as we find him hard at the wine-jar at the latter date, there can be little doubt that he had never really left off. In December, 1525, however, he had a serious warning; he took fever and dysentery, and began to spit blood. In his alarm he made many virtuous resolutions. 'I knew,' he writes, 'whence this illness proceeded, and what conduct had brought on this chastisement'; and he quotes verses in Arabic and Turki to prove the sure penalty of breaking a vow. 'I now once more composed myself to penitence and self-control; I resolved to abstain from such idle thoughts and unseemly pleasures,' and even to renounce poetry and break his pen, in contrition for the quantity of frivolous verse he had thoughtlessly scribbled. But two or three days later he was better, and was so charmed with the view of the camp-fires flickering in the valley beneath his tent one night, that he felt that a libation was distinctly due to the scenery.

Bábar's revels would be merely gross and revolting

but for this touch of romance and sentiment. His enjoyment of wine was but a part of his delight in everything that was beautiful, everything that heightened the quickness of the senses and touched the emotions. On the side of a hill near Kábul he built a little cistern of red granite, which was filled from time to time with red wine. Here he would sit and drink, while the fairest maidens sang and danced around. On the sides of the cistern were chiselled these lines:—

> Sweet is the New Year's coming,
> Sweet the smiling Spring,
> Sweet is the juice of the mellow grape,
> Sweeter far the voice of Love.
> O Bábar, seize life's pleasures,
> Which, once departed, can never, alas! return.

It was not till February 25, 1527, that he carried his good resolution into effect, and, once made, the reform was final. He was near Síkri, preparing for the decisive battle with Ráná Sanga, when, perhaps as a prophylactic or propitiation to the God of Victories, who could scarcely favour a Muslim who indulged in forbidden vice, he suddenly determined to carry out his long-deferred repentance. He sent for all his gold and silver drinking cups, and smashed them in pieces, and gave the fragments to the poor. 'I renounced the use of wine,' he said, 'purifying my mind.' Three hundred of his followers did the like, and the store of wine in the camp was poured out upon the earth, and an almshouse was built upon the spot. An eloquent imperial rescript was indited by Shaikh Zain-ad-dín, calling upon the people, in florid rhetoric, to follow this example, so that 'in all the regions protected by our sway, God keeping watch to guard them from all evil and enmity, there may not be a creature who shall indulge in intoxicating liquor, or employ himself in procuring or making spirits or in selling them, or who shall purchase them, keep them, or carry them out or bring them in.' To signalize this great reform Bábar remitted the *tamgha*, or stamp-tax, from all Muslims throughout his dominions. He never took wine again.

Some notice of Bábar's intemperance is essential in any sketch of his life. For many years it was a prominent part of his daily routine, and fills the largest place in his diary. Without attempting to moralize, we may remark that drunkenness was the hereditary vice of his race and his family, that he did not succumb to it till he was near thirty, and that he made the grand renunciation, which to many men seems to be impossible, at the age of forty-four. It will have been noticed too that he always tippled in company, in a jolly group of 'noble and illustrious drinkers,' after a healthy Rabelaisian fashion, and evidently regarded the wine as an accessory, though a most necessary and delightful accessory, to a merry meeting. His intemperance was really a part of his gay, genial, sunny nature. He was *bon camarade* to his many friends, and among them it was a mark of good comradeship to pledge one another in the bowl.

If he often degraded himself in times of idleness, he knew how to stop when there was work afoot, and he was able to conquer his vice in a supreme and final act of penitence.

The events of 1520–1525 may be passed over rapidly. We have not the brilliant illumination of the Memoirs for these years, and the records of other historians are meagre. Two changes materially strengthened Bábar's position: on the death of his cousin Khán Mirza in 1520, the Emperor's eldest son, Humáyún, was appointed to the government of Badakhshán, and Bábar himself visited this province, accompanied by the young prince's mother; and in September, 1522, Kandahár, which he had long sought to annex, and had lately besieged twice, was surrendered to him by the Arghún chief, Sháh Beg, who had found the Emperor a dangerous neighbour, and so had sought a new province to rule in Sind. Bábar's territory now extended from the Upper Oxus to the Garmsír or 'hot region' on the Persian frontier; he was in no risk of attack upon his flanks, and could advance upon India with security. He had indeed twice made incursions[1] into the Panjáb since his first

[1] Authorities differ about the enumeration of Bábar's invasions of India, though all agree in making them five, as stated in his own Memoirs. Some reckon the early reconnaissance, or tour of inspection in 1505, as the first invasion, though he did not cross the Indus. Bábar himself clearly regarded the Bajaur and Bhira expedition of 1519 as the first invasion; but the break in his Memoirs from January, 1520, to November, 1525, leaves some uncertainty about the second and third, and indeed Erskine casts doubt upon the second altogether.

annexation of Bhíra; but of the second raid we know nothing very certainly; and the third, in 1520, when he again marched through the Gakars' country, punished the rebels who had revolted in and about Bhíra, and pushed on to Siálkót, was abruptly checked by news of an attack on his territory by the Arghúns of Kandahár, which caused his immediate return, and led to the subjugation of that city. It was not till 1524 that he entered resolutely upon the campaigns which ended in the conquest of Hindústán.

CHAPTER XII

PÁNÍPAT

1524–1526

When Bábar at last invaded India in force he was attacking an organized kingdom. It was no longer a case of wild Mongol or Uzbeg tribes; he had to face a settled civilization supported by a disciplined and numerous army. Since the time, five hundred years before, when Mahmúd of Ghazni first carried the standards of Islám over northern India, and left a permanent lodgement in the Panjáb to his successors, six dynasties had upheld the Muhammadan rule in Hindústán, and had extended its sway from Multán to the Gulf of Bengal, and from the Himálayas to the Vindhya mountains, and even into parts of the Deccan. The last of these dynasties, that of the Lódi Afgháns, was now represented by Sultán Ibráhím, who ruled a considerable kingdom from his capital at Delhi. It was, however, greatly shrunk in comparison with former centuries. The rise of independent states had cut off Bengal, Jaunpúr, Málwa, and Gujarát, from the parent crown, and though the 'Kings of the East' had lately been dethroned and their state of Jaunpúr recovered, the King of Delhi was by no means the king of all Muhammadan India, to say nothing of the powerful Rájpút principalities. Sikandar Lódi, the father of Ibráhím, however, had been a vigorous ruler, and had annexed territories to the east and south, and compelled some of the Hindú Rájas to pay him homage; so that he left his son an extended realm, including what we now call the Panjáb, North-West Provinces and Oudh, Bihár, and a portion even of Rájpútána. The organization of the kingdom, however, made against unity. It was parcelled into innumerable principalities and fiefs (*jágírs*), ruled by hereditary chieftains, or by *zemíndárs* appointed from Delhi, all of which tended to create a separate loyalty and obedience, apart from the supreme power. The great fiefs were in the hands of leading Afgháns, and the race is not celebrated for subordination. The early events of Sultán Ibráhím's reign (1518 ff.) had increased the tendency to separation. The kingdom had been divided between him and his brother; civil war was the result, the Amírs had taken sides, and when victory declared for Ibráhím, his severe treatment of many of the Afghán chiefs stirred up general disaffection. Whole provinces rose in revolt, and among them was the Panjáb, whose powerful governor, Daulat Khán, declared his independence.

At this juncture, a royal prince of the Delhi house, 'Alá-ad-dín, commonly called 'Alam-Khán, uncle of Sultán Ibráhím, fled to Bábar at Kábul and entreated him to help him to the throne of his ancestors. Hardly had he made his appeal when Daulat Khán invited the Emperor to come to his aid in the Panjáb. No more propitious moment could be desired. India was seething with faction and discontent; Bábar was strong and prepared, and at his side was a member of the Lódi family to sanction his plans and invite adhesion. The Emperor was soon on the march, and following his previous route to Bhíra was quickly in the neighbourhood of Lahore. The insurgent governor, Daulat Khán, had already been driven out by the Delhi army, but he was amply avenged by the Kábul troops, who routed the enemy with heavy slaughter, and chased them through the streets of Lahore, plundering and burning the bazar. Bábar only rested four days in the capital of the Panjáb, and then pressed on at his best speed to Dibálpúr, where he stormed and sacked the town, and massacred the garrison. Here Daulat Khán joined him; but suspicion of the governor's good faith was aroused, and though treated leniently, he was so little satisfied with the minor fief allotted him by his ally, instead of the whole province, that he fled to the hills to mature plans of vengeance. This defection, natural enough in the circumstances, brought Bábar back from his march upon Delhi. The Panjáb must be secured against its old governor before any further advance could be risked. He appointed some of his most trusty officers to defend the province, and having established 'Sultán' 'Alá-ad-dín at Dibálpúr (with a veteran Mongol to watch him), the Emperor returned to Kábul to beat up reinforcements.

The moment Bábar was out of the way, Daulat Khán took the field, drove 'Alá-ad-dín out of Dibálpúr, and compelled the Turkish officers to concentrate at Lahore. 'Alá-ad-dín fled straight to Kábul, where he offered to cede to Bábar the Panjáb if he would aid him in seizing the throne of Delhi. The treaty was arranged; and armed with the Emperor's promise of immediate support, the pretender hastened back to Lahore. Bábar himself was delayed by some trouble on the Uzbeg border, but set out on his fifth and last invasion of India in November, 1525. His eldest son, Humáyún, brought a contingent from Badakhshán, and Khwája Kalán, trustiest of generals, led the troops of Ghazni. It was the largest army Bábar had ever commanded in Hindústán, yet the total muster, including camp followers, did not exceed twelve thousand men. On crossing the Jhílam he was joined by part of the Lahore army, which had been seriously weakened by an ill-advised march, under 'Alá-ad-dín, upon Delhi, ending in a panic and disgraceful flight. Siálkót had been lost, and Bábar's generals were assembled at Lahore in the hope of making a stand. Daulat Khán, after deceiving 'Alá-ad-dín with pretended support, was now in the field at the head of 40,000 men, and the old Afghán had girded on two swords in token of his resolve to win or die. Nevertheless this valiant army broke and vanished at Bábar's approach. When he reached the banks of the Rávi, where the enemy's camp had been, he found no one to oppose him. A light detachment was sent in pursuit of the fugitives, and the old Khán was compelled to surrender himself, with the two swords still hanging round his neck. It was the last appearance of Daulat Khán, for though his conqueror contented himself with administering a severe upbraiding, and spared his life, the old man died on his way to his village.

Having disposed of this double traitor, and restored order in the Panjáb, the Emperor continued his march towards Delhi, attended by 'Alá-ad-dín, whom, so long as he was useful, he treated with politic respect. Proceeding by way of Sirhind and Ambála, in February, he learned that Sultán Ibráhím was already coming to meet him, supported by a second force from Hisár-Firúza. This latter was effectually dispersed by Humáyún, in his maiden battle; the town was plundered, and Bábar had a hundred prisoners shot, as a warning to the enemy. Heartened by this little victory, he went on by Sháhábád, and followed the Jamna for two marches, till he came within touch of the enemy. It is characteristic that even at this momentous crisis of his career, Bábar found time to visit a fountain at Sirsáwa, 'rather a pretty place,' and to cruise in a boat on the river under an awning, not without the solace of a drug. But he was keenly on the alert, and sent a strong detachment across the river to dislodge the King of Delhi's cavalry outpost, which was driven in and pursued to the edge of the royal camp, with the loss of some elephants and prisoners (April 1).

The decisive battle was fought on April 21st, 1526, on the plain at Pánípat—the historic site where the throne of India has been thrice won. For several days Bábar was busy with his preparations; he collected seven hundred gun-carts, and formed a laager by linking them together with twisted bull-hides, to break a cavalry charge, and by arranging hurdles or shields (*túra*) between each pair to protect the matchlock men[1]. Then two marches more brought

[1] At first sight it seems improbable that Bábar could have possessed seven hundred mounted field pieces, and this led M. Pavet de Courteille (*Mém.*, ii. 273) to dissent from Erskine's rendering 'gun-carriages,' and to substitute 'chariots.' The question, however, is definitely set at rest by the following passage in the *Tarikh-i-Rashidi* (474), where Mirza Haidar describes, as an eye-witness, the artillery of Humáyún's army at the great battle with Shír Khán at Kanauj in May, 1540—only fourteen years after the victory at Pánípat: 'Among the equipments,' he says, 'which were in the train of the Emperor were seven hundred carriages (*gardún*), each drawn by four pair of bullocks, and carrying a swivel (*zarb-zan*) which discharged a ball (*kalola*) of 500 *miskáls* weight [about 5¼ lbs. av.]. . . . And there were twenty-one carriages, each drawn by eight pair of bullocks. Stone balls were of no use in these, but the shot were of molten brass weighing 5,000 *miskáls* [52 lbs.], and the cost of each was 200 *miskáls* of silver. They would strike anything visible at the distance of a *farsakh* [? 4 miles]. . . . The proper plan would be for us to place the mortars and swivels in front; and the gunners, nearly 5,000 in number, must be stationed with the guns. . . . The carriages and mortars and small guns were placed in the centre. The command of the guns was given to Muhammad Khán Rúmi, to the sons of Ustád 'Ali Kúli, to Ustád Ahmad Rúmi, and Husain Khalífa. They placed the carriages and mortars in their proper position, and stretched chains between them.' Baggage-wagons were probably used to supplement gun-carriages in forming a breastwork. Bábar frequently mentions that the arrangement of his chained carriages was copied from the 'Rúmi,' i.e. Osmánli,

the army to Pánípat. Here he stationed the army in such a way that he had the town on his right; his centre was formed by the cannon and matchlocks; and the left was strengthened by ditches and abatis of trees. He was careful to leave gaps in his line a bowshot apart, through which a hundred or a hundred and fifty men could charge abreast.

In spite of every careful disposition, and the confidence in their general which long experience had confirmed, Bábar's men were far from cool. They were months' journeys distant from their homes—always an unsettling reflection in an Oriental army—and in front of them the King of Delhi was believed to muster a hundred thousand troops, with nearly a hundred elephants. On the other hand, Sultán Ibráhím was no match in generalship for Bábar, who describes him contemptuously as 'an inexperienced young man, careless in his movements, who marched without order, halted or retired without

order of battle. Now at the battle of Khaldirán in 1514, between the Osmánlis and the Persians, the former not only chained their guns together, but 'set up their usual breastwork of baggage-wagons and camels in front of the Janizaries' (Hammer, *Geschichte des Osmanischen Reiches*, i. 717). The Osmánlis, therefore, used a wagon laager in the centre as well as chained guns at the extremities of their line of battle, and Bábar probably copied both arrangements. Mr. Oman tells me that the use of war-carts, formed and manœuvred in hollow squares, was invented by the Hussites in the Bohemian wars to resist the German cavalry. The horses were taken out and the carts chained together on the approach of the enemy, and men with hand-guns were mounted on the carts. The Osmánlis doubtless copied the Bohemians, and handed on the idea to the Persians, and thence to Bábar.

method, and engaged without foresight.' The fact that the invaders were suffered to go on entrenching themselves at Pánípat for over a week without molestation was proof of the incompetence as well as the timidity of the enemy, who even suffered a little band of the imperial troops to insult them by riding up to their camp and shooting arrows into it, with perfect impunity. That week, when the two armies lay facing each other, was wholly in Bábar's favour: it gave his men time to recover confidence.

On the 20th of April a night surprise was attempted upon the enemy's position, and though it failed, owing to the confusion of the troops in the darkness, it had the effect of drawing the enemy out of his camp. Sultán Ibráhím, elated by the ease with which this attack had been driven back, brought his army out at dawn on the 21st in battle array. The moment Bábar detected the movement of the enemy, his men were ordered to put on their helmets and mail, and take up their stations. His army was drawn up behind his laager in the usual order, right and left centre, right and left wing, advance guard, and reserve; but in addition he had placed flanking parties of Mongols on the extreme right and left, with orders to execute their famous national manœuvre, the *tulughma*—that rapid wheel, charging the enemy's rear, of which Bábar had himself proved only too thoroughly the tremendous effect.

The army of Delhi came straight on, at a quick march, without a halt from the start. They seemed to be aiming at Bábar's right, and he sent up the reserve to its support. As the enemy came up to the ditches, abatis, and hurdles, they hesitated, and the pressure of the troops behind threw them into some confusion. Taking advantage of this, Bábar sent out his Mongol flankers through the gaps in the laager, and they galloped round the enemy and poured their arrows into the rear. Part of the Emperor's left wing, advancing incautiously, got into difficulties; but the general's eye was on them, and they were promptly supported from the centre. Meanwhile the right was also hard pressed, and Bábar sent forward his right centre to their assistance. The master gunner, Ustád 'Ali, made pretty practice with his *feringi* pieces, in front of the line, and was admirably seconded by Mustafá, the cannoneer on the left centre. The enemy was now engaged on all sides, front, flanks, and rear; and their charges, which seemed ineffective to men who had stood up to the Mongols' swoop, were easily repulsed and driven back upon their centre, which was already too crowded to be able to use its strength. In this jammed confusion they lay at the mercy of the hardy Turks and Mongols, who fell upon the strangled ranks with deadly effect. By noon the great army of the King of Delhi was broken and flying for dear life. Sultán Ibráhím himself lay stark on the field, amidst some fifteen thousand of his dead. They brought his head to Bábar; and prisoners, elephants, and spoil of all sorts began to come in from the pursuers. 'The sun had mounted spear-high when the onset began, and the battle lasted till mid-day, when the enemy were completely broken and routed, and my people victorious and triumphant. By the grace and mercy of Almighty God this difficult affair was made easy to me, and that mighty army, in the space of half a day, was laid in the dust.' Two detachments were at once dispatched to occupy Delhi and Agra, and on Friday, April 27, the public prayer was said in the mosque of the capital in the name of the new Emperor, the first of the 'Great Moghuls.'

The whole thing had been almost incredibly easy. Seldom was a day—

So fought, so followed, and so fairly won.

The explanation is no doubt to be found partly in the unpopularity of Sultán Ibráhím, whose severity and avarice, joined to military incapacity, fostered treachery, or at least half-heartedness, among his troops. We read of no actual desertions, and many of his men fought to the death; but there must have been disaffection, as well as a want of confidence in their leader, to allow 100,000 well-armed troops to go down, break, and run, before an army one-tenth their size. Bábar's generalship, however, had much to do with the successful issue. His skilful disposition of his men behind a fortified laager, which checked the enemy's charges, above all their heavy elephants; his adoption of the Mongol flanking manœuvre; and his alert support of each section of his line the instant he detected any wavering—

these were among the causes of his victory. His men began the battle in no little alarm: it was their Emperor's cool science and watchful tactics that restored their confidence and gave them back their pluck.

To the Afgháns of Delhi the battle of Pánípat was their Cannae. It was the ruin of their dominion, the end of their power. In their despair they raised their dead Sultán, poor creature as he was, to the sanctity of a martyr, and long continued to make pilgrimages to his grave. The battlefield became an uncanny spot which no man cared to pass after dark. Wailing and groans and other supernatural sounds were heard there of nights; and the historian Badáóni, a man of veracity in his way, crossing the haunted plain one night with some friends, heard the dreadful voices, and fell to repeating the holy names of God as a protection from the awful influences around him.

Bábar had his share of superstition, but he was too busy at first to think of it. He was gathering such spoil as passed all dreams. He had seized the royal treasuries at Delhi and Agra, and the first business was to divide the booty among the expectant troops. To Humáyún, who had played his part like a man in the great battle, he gave seventy lakhs (of dáms, i.e. about £20,000) and a treasure which no one had counted. His chief Begs were rewarded with six to ten lakhs apiece (£1,700 to £2,800). Every man who had fought received his share, and even the traders and camp-followers were remembered in the general bounty. Besides this, the Emperor's other sons and relations, though absent, had presents of gold and silver, cloth and jewels, and captive slaves. Friends in Fargháná, Khurásán, Káshghar, and Persia were not forgotten; and holy men in Herát and Samarkand, and Mekka and Medina, received substantial offerings. Finally, to every person in Kábul, man, woman, slave and free, young or old, a silver coin was sent in celebration of the victory. The balance was stored in the treasury to carry on the government and support the army.

For himself, Bábar kept nothing. When Humáyún brought him the glorious diamond, one of the famous historical jewels, valued at 'half the daily expenditure of the whole world,' which the family of the late Rája Bikramajit had given him in gratitude for his chivalrous protection, the father gave it back to the young prince[1]. He had no love for wealth or precious stones, except to give away, and his prodigal

[1] Mr. H. Beveridge (*Calcutta Review*, 1897) quotes a passage from a MS. by Sháh Khúr Sháh, in the British Museum (Or. 153), in which it is related how Humáyún presented this famous diamond to Sháh Tahmásp, who 'did not value it so highly,' and sent it as a gift to the Nizám Sháh in the Deccan. Mr. Beveridge conjectures that this diamond may be identical with that (the 'Great Mogul') presented to Sháh Jahán, i.e. the Koh-i-Núr. It is a remarkable point that Bábar gives the weight of his diamond as 8 *miskáls* or 320 *ratis*, and that Tavernier states the weight of the 'Great Mogul' diamond to be $319\frac{1}{2}$ *ratis*. See V. Ball's Appendix I to vol. ii of his translation of Tavernier's *Travels*. But Professor Ball did not know that Bábar's diamond had been sent back to the Deccan.

generosity in distributing the immense spoil of the Delhi kings gained him the nickname of 'the Kalandar'—the beggar-friar. He had what he prized far above jewels and gold. He had renown and a name in history for all time.

CHAPTER XIII

HINDÚSTÁN

1526–1528

BÁBAR was now king of Delhi, but not yet king of Hindústán, much less of India. Even of the dominion of Delhi, which then stretched from the Indus to Bihár, and from Gwáliár to the Himálayas, he was only nominally master. The Lódi dynasty, indeed, was dethroned, and its last king slain, but that king left a brother to claim the crown, and the land remained unsubdued east and south of Agra. The people were hostile to the strangers of uncouth tongue, and each town and petty ruler prepared for obstinate resistance. The country round Agra was in open revolt. Biána, Mewát, Dholpúr, Gwáliár, Ráberi, Etáwa, Kálpi, were all fortifying against attack, unanimous in rejecting the newcomers. In spite of the surfeit of treasure, Bábar's troops were like to starve. 'When I came to Agra,' he says, 'it was the hot season. All the inhabitants fled from terror, so that we could find neither grain for ourselves nor fodder for our beasts. The villages, out of mere hatred and spite to us, had taken to anarchy, thieving, and marauding. The roads became impassable. I had not had time, after the division of the treasure, to send fit persons to occupy and protect the different pargánas and stations. The heats this year chanced to be unusually oppressive, and many men dropped at about the same time, as though struck by the *samúm*, and died on the spot.'

The troops began to murmur. They longed for the cool air of Kábul, and even made ready for return. They looked upon India 'as a buccaneer looked on a galleon'; the prize-money distributed, they wished to make sail. Bábar was exceedingly angry, especially when the grumbling of the rank and file reached his ears. He could take advice, on occasion, from his Begs, tried warriors, and politic men of affairs:—but this rabble! 'Where was the sense or decency of eternally dinning the same tale in the ears of one who saw the facts with his own eyes, and had formed a calm and fixed resolve in regard to the business in hand? What use was there in the whole army, down to the very dregs, giving their stupid uninformed opinions?' He was bitterly disappointed at their want of loyal confidence. Even Khwája Kalán, his best general, whose six brothers had followed him to their deaths, was eager to return home.

They had to deal with an obstinate man, however, and Bábar soon showed them his mettle. He summoned the Begs to a council, and spoke his mind. He recalled the toils and labours of the past years, the weary marches and grievous hardships, and reminded them that all these had been endured for the sake of the great reward which was now theirs. 'A mighty enemy had been overcome, and a rich and powerful kingdom was at their feet. And now, having attained our goal and won our game, are we to turn back from all we have accomplished and fly to Kábul like men who have lost and are discomfited? Let no man who calls himself my friend ever again moot such a thing. But if there be any one of you who cannot bring himself to stay, then let him go.' Thoroughly shamed, the murmurers dared not say a word: the whole army returned to its senses. So the plague of disaffection was stayed among the people. Only Khwája Kalán was sent as governor to Ghazni, because a man of his influence and ability was needed to protect the country. Bábar, however, was deeply offended with his veteran officer, and the offence was doubled when the Khwája, who was a cultivated man, wrote these lines on a wall at Delhi:—

> If safe and sound I pass the Sind,
> Damned if I ever wish for Hind.

Bábar in reply sent him the verse:—

> Bábar! give all thanks that the favour of God Most High
> Hath given thee Sind and Hind and widespread royalty:
> If the heats of India make thee long for the mountain cold,
> Remember the frost and ice that numbed thee in Ghazni of old!

There are few acts more splendidly heroic in Bábar's career than this bold resolution to stay where he was, in the middle of India, among hostile nations and a discontented soldiery. And the reward of firmness soon appeared. He had not only won over his own army but many of his enemies. The people had imagined that his invasion was no more than a temporary raid, like his ancestor Tímúr's, and thought that he would depart as soon as he was gorged with treasure. To such a robber they would offer strenuous resistance. But when they found that he had come to live amongst them, they began to examine him more curiously, and to consider what policy was likely to pay. All they could learn about the new conqueror was in his favour. His severities were as nothing compared with his generous magnanimity. His courage and generalship were proved, and if he meant to stay and rule the land, who was there fit to be weighed in the balance against him? Tired of the barbarities and uneasiness of civil war, recognizing no chief of Bábar's level, the fighting men who had long trampled on Hindústán began to see the merits of a master. The tide of public opinion turned and set steadily towards Bábar's side.

First an Afghán officer came over with a valuable contingent of two or three thousand retainers from the Doáb. Then a powerful chief was won by the Emperor's clemency to his captured sons. Still more wonderful was the submission of the whole Afghán army, which the late king of Delhi had dispatched to subdue the revolted province of Bihár. They one and all acclaimed the new order, and Bábar, by a stroke of genius, rewarded them with the gift of valuable fiefs in the parts of Jaunpúr and Oudh which were still in revolt. Naturally the prospect of handsome revenues spurred on their energies. Meanwhile Sambhal was taken by guile; and Humáyún led an army against the insurgent Afgháns in the east, who were advancing into the Doáb, but immediately broke up on his approach and fled over the Ganges. The young prince pursued, took Jaunpúr and Gházípúr, and leaving strong divisions in Jaunpúr and Oudh, marched back by way of Kálpi to support his father against a pressing danger. For Bábar was now coming to the grip with the only formidable rival left in Hindústán, the great Ráná Sanga of Chítór.

'Ráná Sanga was the head of the Rájpút principality of Chítór, now known as Udaipúr, and the representative of a family which, by the universal consent of the Rájpúts, is allowed the pre-eminence among all the Rájpút tribes as the most ancient and the noblest. Like Bábar, he had been educated in the school of adversity. After overcoming the many difficulties and dangers of his early life, when he at length mounted the throne he carried on successful wars with his neighbours on every side, and added largely to his hereditary dominions. From Sultán Mahmúd Khilji, the king of Málwa—whom he defeated in battle, took prisoner, and honourably entertained in a spirit worthy of the best days of chivalry—he had wrested the wide and valuable provinces of Bhílsa, Sárangpúr, Chánderi and Rántbór. He had engaged in hostilities with Sultán Ibráhím of Delhi, and twice had met the Sultán himself in pitched battles. "Eighty thousand horse, seven Rájas of the highest rank, nine Raos, and one hundred and four chieftains bearing the titles of Ráwul and Ráwut, with five hundred war elephants, followed him into the field. The princes of Márwár and Ambér did him homage, and the Raos of Gwáliár, Ajmír, Síkri, Raesen, Kalpek, Chánderi, Búndi, Gagraon, Rámpúra, and Abú, served him as tributaries or held of him in chief." His personal figure corresponded with his deeds. "He exhibited at his death but the fragment of a warrior; one eye was lost in the broil with his brother, an arm in an action with the Lódi King of Delhi, and he was a cripple owing to a limb being broken with a cannon-ball in another, while he counted eighty wounds from the sword or the lance on various parts of his body." And his rival, Bábar, who loved in an enemy the qualities he himself possessed, pays him only a just tribute of respect when he says that the high eminence he then held he had attained but recently by his valour and his sword[1].'

The two men belonged to widely different races—Bábar, the Turco-Mongolian of Western Tartary, Sanga, the pure Aryan of the East: but each recognized his rival's greatness, for—

> There is neither East nor West,
>   Border nor Breed nor Birth,
> When two strong men stand face to face,
>   Tho' they come from the ends of the earth.

The Ráná had even sent a complimentary embassy to Bábar at Kábul, offering to join in the attack on

[1] Erskine, *History of India*, i. 460, 461; Tod's *Rajasthan*, ii. 229, 307.

the Delhi kingdom. When the time came, however, he thought better of it, and Bábar resented the defection. On his side the Rájpút claimed territory on the western bank of the Ganges, which Bábar had occupied. One of these places was Biána, which was too near Agra to be left unsubdued. Tardi Beg, whom we have met before in different circumstances, was sent to seize the fort, and though the first attempt was an egregious failure, the Muhammadan commander of Biána, hearing that Ráná Sanga was coming to the rescue, preferred surrendering to his fellow Muslims to yielding the fortress to a Hindú 'pagan.' In the same way, and for the same cause, Dholpúr opened its gates to the Emperor's troops, and finally Gwáliár, the famous fortress on its impregnable crag, was taken by stratagem.

This was coming to close quarters; and soon after Humáyún had brought back his army to Agra, Bábar learnt without surprise that the Ráná was marching on Biána, and had been joined by Hasan Khán of Mewát. It was war to the knife. The Emperor lost no time, but sending on a light detachment towards the threatened fortress, with orders to hang on the enemy and harass him, he set out himself with his main body in battle array on February 11, 1527. All his campaigns hitherto had been against fellow Muslims; now, for the first time, he was marching against 'heathens'; it was the *Jihád*, the holy war. Moreover, these 'heathens' were fighting-men of the first class. Bábar had some experiences of the warlike capacities of various races. He knew the Mongol wheeling swoop, the Uzbeg charge, the Afghán skirmish, and the steady fighting of his own Turks; but he was now to meet warriors of a higher type than any he had encountered. 'The Rájpúts, energetic, chivalrous, fond of battle and bloodshed, animated by a strong national spirit, were ready to meet face to face the boldest veterans of the camp, and were at all times prepared to lay down their life for their honour.' Their chivalry and lofty sense of honour inspired nobler feats and sacrifices than any that were conceived by Bábar's less highly wrought soldiers.

The Emperor camped at Síkri—afterwards Akbar's exquisite palace-city of Fathpúr—where he was joined by the garrison from Biána. These men had already received a lesson from the Rájpúts, of whose bravery and daring they all spoke in unmeasured praise. The enemy was evidently not one that could be trifled with. An outpost affair soon confirmed this impression: an incautious advance by one of the Amírs was at once detected by the Rájpúts, who sent the Turks flying back to camp with some loss, including a standard. The pursuers only pulled up when they came in sight of a strong detachment which Bábar had quickly sent out to cover the retreat. Being now in touch with the enemy, the Emperor put his army in battle array. As before at Pánípat, he ranged the gun-carriages, and probably the baggage wagons, so as to cover his front, and chained them together at a distance of five paces. Mustafá, from Turkey, ordered his artillery admirably in the Ottoman manner on the left wing, but Ustád 'Ali had a different method. Where there were no guns or wagons, a ditch was dug, backed by portable wooden tripods on wheels, lashed together at a few paces apart. These preparations took twenty-five days, and were designed to restore the confidence of the troops. The army, in fact, was almost in a panic at the reports of the numbers and courage of the Rájpúts, and an astrologer —an 'evil-minded rascally fellow'—added to the general uneasiness by his foolish predictions, of which, to his credit, Bábar took no heed. His every energy was bent upon getting the army into a fit state to meet the enemy—'stiffen their sinews, summon up the blood.'

It was at this anxious moment, when his men were quaking in anticipation of the struggle with their unknown foes, that Bábar made his memorable renunciation of wine, broke his drinking cups, poured out the stores of liquor on the ground, and promulgated his total-abstinence manifesto to the army. It was a time for solemn vows of reformation, and in common with many of his followers the Emperor adopted the usual token of a pledge, by letting his beard grow. Then he called his dispirited officers together, and addressed them:—

'GENTLEMEN AND SOLDIERS,—"Every man that comes into the world must pass away: God alone is immortal, unchangeable. Whoso sits down to the feast of life must end by drinking the cup of death. All visitors of the inn of mortality must one day leave this house of sorrow." Rather let us die with honour than live disgraced!

> With fame, though I die, I am content,
> Let fame be mine, though life be spent.

God most high has been gracious in giving us this destiny, that if we fall we die martyrs, if we conquer we triumph in His holy cause. Let us swear with one accord by the great name of God that we will never turn back from such a death, or shrink from the stress of battle, till our souls are parted from our bodies.'

Master and servant, great and small, every man seized the Korán and took the oath. After that, the army began to pluck up. They needed it, for every day brought bad news: a fort had surrendered, a chief had turned traitor, a detachment had been forced to retire, the Indians who had joined the army began to desert. Waiting only made the situation worse, and Bábar resolved to advance upon the enemy. On New Year's Day, March 12, he writes:—

'I advanced my wagons [and guns] and tripods with all the apparatus and machines that I had prepared, and marched forward with my army in order of battle—right wing, left wing, and centre in their places. In front were the wagons, gun-carriages, and tripods on wheels, and behind came Ustád 'Ali Kúli, with a body of his matchlock men, to prevent the communication being cut off between the artillery and the infantry behind, and to enable them to advance and form into line. When the ranks were formed and every man in his place, I galloped along the line, encouraging the Begs and men of the centre, right, and left, giving special directions to each division how to act, and to each man orders how to proceed and engage. Then, when all was arranged, I moved the army on in order of battle for a couple of miles, when we camped. The pagans, getting notice of our movements, were on the alert, and several bodies drew out to face us and came close up to our wagons and ditch. . . . I did not intend fighting that day, but sent out a few skirmishers by way of taking an omen. They took a number of pagans and cut off their heads, which they brought in. . . . This raised the spirits of the army wonderfully, and gave them confidence.'

It was not till Saturday, March 16, 1527, that the two armies met at Kanwáha in pitched battle. Bábar had pushed on another mile or two, and was busy setting the camp, when the news came that the enemy were advancing. Instantly every man was sent to his post, the line of chained guns and wagons was strengthened, and the army drawn up for the fight. A special feature in the disposition was the great strength of the reserves. Bábar himself commanded the centre, assisted by his cousin, Chín Tímúr, a son of Ahmad, the late Khán of Mongolistán. Humáyún led the right, and the Emperor's son-in-law, Mahdi Khwája, the left. Among the minor commanders was a grandson of Sultán Husain of Herát; and the Lódi 'Alá-ad-dín, the claimant to the crown of Delhi, whom Bábar still used as a figure-head, had his post. Of the number of the imperial troops there is no estimate, but the Rájpúts were credited with over 200,000—probably a rough guess, based upon the known maximum of Rájpút levies; but Ráná Sanga evidently had a very powerful following. The chiefs of Bhílsa, rated at 30,000 horse, of Mewát, Dongarpúr, and Chánderi, with about 12,000 each, brought the flower of Rájpút chivalry at their backs; and Mahmúd Lódi, brother of the late Sultán Ibráhím, another claimant to the throne, had collected a body of 10,000 mercenaries to support his pretensions. Whatever the exact numbers, 'a more gallant army could not be brought into the field.'

'The battle began, about half-past nine in the morning, by a desperate charge made by the Rájpúts on Bábar's right. Bodies of the reserve were pushed on to its assistance; and Mustafá Rúmi, who commanded one portion of the artillery [and matchlocks] on the right of the centre, opened a fire upon the assailants. Still, new bodies of the enemy poured on undauntedly, and new detachments from the reserve were sent to resist them. The battle was no less desperate on the left, to which also it was found necessary to dispatch repeated parties from the reserve. When the battle had lasted several hours, and still continued to rage, Bábar sent orders to the flanking columns to wheel round and charge; and he soon after ordered the guns to advance, and, by a simultaneous movement, the household troops and cavalry stationed behind the cannon were ordered to gallop out on right and left of the matchlock men in the centre, who also moved forward and continued their fire, hastening to fling themselves with all their fury on the enemy's centre. When this was observed in the wings they also advanced. These unexpected movements, made at the same moment, threw the enemy into confusion. Their centre was shaken; the men who were displaced by the attack made in flank on the wings and rear were forced upon the centre and crowded together. Still the gallant Rájpúts were not appalled. They made repeated desperate attacks on the Emperor's centre, in hopes of recovering the day; but were bravely and steadily received, and swept away in great numbers. [Ustád 'Ali's "huge balls" did fearful execution among the "heathen."] Towards evening the confusion was complete, and the slaughter was consequently dreadful. The fate of the battle was decided. Nothing remained for the Rájpúts but to force their way through the bodies of the enemy that were now in their rear, and to effect a retreat. The Emperor pursued them as far as their camp, and . . . detached a strong body of horse with orders to pursue the broken troops of the confederates without halting; to cut up all they met, and to prevent them from reassembling[1].'

The victory was final, complete. The enemy fled in all directions, leaving multitudes of slain upon the fields and roads around. Many chiefs had fallen, and the heads of gallant Rájpúts rose in the ghastly tower erected by their conqueror, who now took the title he had earned of *Gházi*, or Victor in the Holy War. Indeed, had Bábar pressed the pursuit he would have almost exterminated the Rájpút power, and *ultimus ille dies bello gentique fuisset*. As it was, the noble Sanga himself escaped, though severely wounded, but from that day forth no Ráná of his line

[1] This is Erskine's abridgement of the account of the battle given in the official dispatch. The dispatch was written by Shaikh Zain-ed-din, in the ornate style that Persians admire, and is a model of obscurity. Tod's *Rajasthán* i, 305–6, gives the Rájpút account, from which it appears that, during the long wait at Síkri, Bábar proposed terms to the Ráná and even offered to pay him an annual tribute. Confident of victory, Sanga declined the proposals. The Rájpúts attributed their defeat to the treachery of one of their chiefs.

ever took the field in person against an Emperor of Bábar's house. Within a year the invader had struck two decisive blows, which shattered the power of two great organized forces. The battle of Pánípat had utterly broken the power of the Muhammadan Afgháns in India; the battle of Kanwáha crushed the great confederacy of the Hindús.

But Bábar had not done with the Rájpúts yet. He had beaten them, but he meant also to punish them. When his troops mustered again in winter after the rainy season, he resolved to lead them into the enemy's country and attack one of their chief strongholds. He marched against Chánderi, on the south-east of Málwa, the fastness of Medíni Rao, one of the Rána's distinguished lieutenants, king-maker in Málwa, and head of the Rájpúts of that part. His way took him down the Jamna, which he crossed below the confluence of the Chambal, to Kálpi, whence he diverged towards his goal, cutting a path through the jungle for his guns and wagons. He reached Chánderi on January 20, 1528. Medíni Rao was in his fortress with some five thousand of his gallant followers, and proudly rejected Bábar's offer of terms. Just as the besiegers were closing round the place, the prime minister, Nizám-ad-dín Khalífa, brought the Emperor the disturbing news that the army he had sent against the Afgháns of Bihár had been defeated, and abandoning Lucknow was falling back on Kanauj. Seeing Khalífa's perturbation, Bábar remarked reassuringly that all things were in God's hands, and there was no use in anxiety;

he bade his minister conceal the bad news, and strain every nerve to carry Chánderi by assault in the morning. The outer fort was taken in the night[1]. In the morning a general assault was ordered, and in spite of the stones and fire which the Rájpúts threw down on their heads, the storming parties gained the walls in several places and seized a covered way that led to the citadel. The upper fort was quickly forced, and the desperate Rájpúts, seeing that all was lost, killed all their women and children, and rushing out naked, fell furiously upon the Muslims, slaughtered as many as they could, and then threw themselves over the ramparts. A remnant had gathered in Medíni Rao's house, where they slew each other with enthusiasm: 'one man took his stand with a sword, and others came pressing on, one by one, and stretched out their necks, eager to die; in this way many went to hell.' To Bábar this desperate sacrifice appeared only an exhibition of pagan infatuation, and he piled up the heads of these heroic suicides in a tower on a hill-top without a word of admiration for their gallant end. He was only surprised at the ease with which in the space of an hour, and without his full strength, he had stormed so redoubtable a fortress.

Soon after this second blow, the great Ráná Sanga,

[1] Kháfi Khán, a late authority, says that the outer fort (including the town) was surrendered on condition that the garrison and inhabitants would be spared, but that the Rájpúts broke the peace, and the Muslims thereupon slew some thousands and assaulted the citadel as described above.

Bábar's only comparable rival, died, and a contest over the succession deprived the Rájpút confederacy of any leader. There was no more trouble with the Hindús in his time, but that time was short. The mighty Mongol was soon to join the gallant Rájpút among the shades.

CHAPTER XIV

EMPIRE

1528–30

THE chief work of the remaining two years of Bábar's life was to quench the last sparks of rebellion. We have said nothing so far about the organization or polity of the empire,—which now stretched from Kunduz and Badakhshán by the Oxus to the borders of Bengal, and from the Himálayas to Gwáliár,—because Bábar had no time to organize. A large part of the Empire was scarcely controlled at all, and the polity of Hindústán under his rule was simply the strong hand of military power where it could be used. The lands and cities of the more settled regions were parcelled out among his officers, or *jágírdárs*, who levied the land-tax from the peasant cultivators, the duties from the merchants and shopkeepers, and the poll-tax from non-Muslims[1]. The great *zamíndárs* or landholders

[1] Bábar gives a list of the imperial revenue derived from the various provinces (including the Cis-Sutlej province, i. e. Bhíra, Lahore, Siálkót, Dibálpúr, &c.; Sírhind, Hisár-Firúza, Dehli, Mewát, Biána, Agra, Mián-i-Viláyat, Gwáliár, Kálpi, Kanauj, Sambhal, Lucknow, Khairábád, Oudh and Baráich, Jaunpúr, Karra and Mánikpúr, Bihár, Sirwár, Chipáran, Gondla; and tribute from Tirhút, Rantambhór, Nágor, and various Rájas), and puts the total at fifty-two crores of *tankas*, which Erskine

were often in but nominal dependence on the crown; and India, as Erskine observes, was 'rather a congeries of little states under one prince, than one regular and uniformly governed kingdom.' The frontier and mountain districts, indeed, could hardly be said to have submitted in more than form; the Afghán tribes were still practically independent; and in Sind on the west, and Bihár on the east, the imperial authority was very lightly recognized.

Bihár gave most trouble. The Afghán insurgents still held out in the eastern part of Bábar's empire, and had even assumed the offensive when they saw him busy with the Rájpút campaigns. Treachery and deserters had swelled their numbers, and they had advanced into the Doáb, stormed Shamsábád, and driven the imperial garrison out of Kanauj. As soon as Chánderi had fallen, Bábar set out (February 2, 1528) to punish their temerity. He crossed the Jamna—an operation which with his large force took several days—and, sending on a light reconnaissance to Kanauj, discovered that the enemy, abandoning the city on the news of his approach, had hurriedly recrossed the Ganges, and were now mustered on the east bank to dispute his passage. The Emperor reached the great river on February 27, and encamped opposite the insurgents. Collecting thirty or forty of the enemy's

is disposed to reckon at £4,212,000. If, however, the *tanka* is taken to be the equivalent of the *dám*, as in Akbar's time, the revenue would be less than £1,500,000. This revenue is solely that derived from the land tax, and does not represent the gross income of the crown.

boats, he ordered a bridge to be thrown across the broad stream. The Afgháns mocked at so wild a project, but the bridge went on; and the skilful fire of the matchlocks and artillery, discharged from an island and from a battery on the bank, protected the engineers who were constructing the pontoon. Ustád 'Ali even succeeded in firing off the big cannon called '*Díg Ghází*' ('Victorious Gun,' a title it had won in the battle of Kanwáha) no less than sixteen times a day, which was clearly a record performance at that time; but a still more ponderous piece unluckily burst at the first discharge.

On March 13 the bridge was finished, and some of the infantry and the Panjáb troops were sent over to skirmish. The next day a large part of the army crossed, and were at once engaged by the Afgháns, who were supported by elephants. Bábar's troops held their footing stubbornly till night, when they crossed back and rejoined the rest of the army on the west bank. On the two following days the artillery and the whole of the imperial forces were safely got across, but the enemy had prudently decamped. They were hotly pursued nearly as far as Oudh, with the loss of their families and baggage, and many were overtaken and slain. The Afghán army was utterly dispersed for the time, and Bábar returned to Agra for the rainy season.

Frequent and prolonged attacks of fever had warned him that the climate of India was not to be trifled with, and his peculiar febrifuge—consisting in translating a religious tract into verse—did not answer his expectations. His wandering, restless life, too, was telling upon his hardy constitution. He notes that since the age of eleven he had never kept the great annual feast after Ramazán twice in the same place. Yet between his fits of fever his vigour remained extraordinary. He had been known to take up a man under each arm, and run with them round the battlements of a fortress, leaping the embrasures; and even in March, 1529, he notes: 'I swam across the river Ganges for amusement. I counted my strokes, and found that I swam over in thirty-three strokes. I then took breath, and swam back to the other side. I had crossed by swimming every river I had met, except only the Ganges.' He was also perpetually in the saddle, riding eighty miles a day sometimes, and the rapidity of his marches was often amazing.

At Agra, in December, he gave a splendid garden entertainment, and the names of the guests show the extent of his power and reputation. There were noted Khwájas from his lost Samarkand, ambassadors from the Uzbeg Sultán, from the Sháh of Persia, and from the King of Bengal, who all received magnificent presents in return for their offerings. A touching part of the ceremony was Bábar's grateful gift of costly dresses and valuables 'to the men who had come from Andiján, who, without a country, without a home, had roamed with me in my wanderings in Súkh and Hushyár and many lands, my tried veterans.' There were fights of camels and elephants and rams, and wrestling matches, to amuse the visitors; and during dinner the Indian jugglers and tumblers performed wonderful tricks, which Bábar had never seen before. Dancing girls added their peculiar charm, and in the evening money was freely scattered in the crowd: 'there was a precious hubbub.'

The city in which he gave this *tamásha* was a very different place from the Agra he had found. His delight in running water had led him to sink wells and build tanks among the tamarinds beside the Jamna, and to lay out gardens, where he planted the rose and narcissus in regular parterres. He employed six hundred and eighty masons daily on his new buildings, and though he confesses that he had to proceed 'without neatness or order, in the Hindú fashion,' yet he 'produced edifices and gardens of very tolerable regularity.' In India a 'garden' includes a dwelling, and Bábar's Chárbágh with its marble pavilions and beds of roses must have been a delightful palace. The Indians, who had never seen this sort of pleasure-ground, called it 'Kábul'; and we may be sure the name carried sweet associations to the designer.

He was not left long in repose. The Afgháns in Bihár were not yet quelled. Mahmúd Lódi, the brother of Sultán Ibráhím, had arrived among them, and they flocked to the standard of their hereditary king. Jaunpúr and most of Bihár declared for him, and the many factions laid aside their rivalries for the moment to support the last chance of an Afghán restoration. Bábar received this news in the middle of January, 1529, whilst he was staying at Dholpúr, preparing for a predatory campaign in the west. He at once returned to Agra and led his army out. On reaching the Ganges he was met by his son 'Askari, whom he had sent on a few weeks before to take the command in the eastern provinces. Having been fully informed as to the situation of the enemy, the Emperor marched down the right bank of the river, while 'Askari's force kept pace with him on the other side, camping opposite his father each night. At the news of his approach the large army of the Afgháns, numbering, it was said, a hundred thousand men, hastened away: the Lódi pretender fled from before Chunár, to which he was laying siege; Shír Khán escaped from Benáres; and as Bábar pressed on past Alláhábád, Chunár, Benáres, and Gházípúr, to Baksar (Buxar), several of the Afghán leaders came in to offer their submission; and Mahmúd, finding himself almost deserted, sought protection with the Bengal army.

The Kingdom of Bengal had long been independent of Delhi, and Bábar had no immediate intention of subduing it, so long as it did not interfere with him. The King, Nasrat Sháh, had sent ambassadors to Agra, who had professed amity, and even paid *pishkash* or tribute; and the reports from Bengal had so far been entirely reassuring. Nevertheless the Bengal troops were now massed on the frontier and were apparently supporting the defeated Afgháns. On the other hand, it was possible that they were merely taking precautions against the war being carried into their own country. An envoy from the King of Bengal was informed that no injury was intended towards his country, but that the Emperor was resolved to quell the rebels wherever they might be found. The envoy departed with the customary gifts and robe of honour, but it became clear that his master meant war. Reinforced by 20,000 men from Jaunpúr, Bábar resolved to force the passage of the Gogra in face of the Bengális. He made unusually elaborate preparations, for he knew the enemy were skilful gunners, and were in great force. Ustád 'Ali was to plant his cannon, *feringi* pieces, and swivels (*zarb-zan*) on a rising ground at the point between the two rivers, and also keep up a hot fire from his matchlock-men upon the Bengáli camp on the east bank of the Gogra. A little below the junction of the rivers, Mustafá was to direct a cannonade from his artillery, supported by matchlocks, on the enemy's flank, and upon the Bengal flotilla which lay off an island. A number of sappers were sent to raise the batteries and set up the guns and ammunition stores. The main army was formed up in six divisions, four of which, under the Emperor's son 'Askari, were already north of the Ganges. These were to cross the Gogra by boats or fords, and keep the enemy busy while the artillery was being carried across, and a strong force was sent ahead to divert their attention. The fifth division under Bábar himself was to cover Ustád 'Ali's batteries above the confluence, and then to cross the Gogra under the cover of the guns; whilst the sixth went to the support of Mustafá's artillery on the right bank of the Ganges.

On Sunday and Monday, May 2 and 3, 1529, these two divisions crossed the Ganges, and on Tuesday they marched on to the Gogra. Ustád 'Ali at the confluence was making excellent practice with his *feringis* upon the Bengal vessels in the river. Bábar, who was suffering, went on board one of his boats, and took a dose of bhang—he had not given up his bolus, as well as his cup. Wednesday was spent in skirmishes with the Bengal boats, (several of which were captured,) in searching for a ford, and preparing for the forcing of the river. Meanwhile news came that 'Askari had got his divisions over the Gogra, and on the morning of Thursday, May 6, the battle began. The Bengal army, as was foreseen, moved up the river to meet 'Askari, and Bábar at once ordered the fifth and sixth divisions to cross anyhow, swimming, in boats, or on bundles of reeds, and take the enemy in the rear. The movement was brilliantly carried out in the face of a determined resistance. Attacked in front and rear and flank, the enemy broke and fled. Good generalship had once more guided valour to victory.

The result was the collapse of the Afghán rebellion, and the conclusion of a treaty of peace with Bengal. In three battles Bábar had reduced northern India to submission.

It was the last exploit of his life: his diary stops

soon afterwards, save for a few fragments. One of the entries shows that he was writing in the midst of his campaigns, for he records how the rainy season burst upon him in a violent storm on May 26, which blew the tent down over his head so suddenly that 'he had not time to gather up his papers and the loose sheets that were written.' 'The books and sheets of paper,' he adds, 'were drenched and wet, but were gathered together with much pains, folded in woollen cloth, and placed under a bed over which carpets were thrown to dry and press them.' We need not follow him on his journey back to Agra. One of the latest notes in the diary mentions his reunion with his wife, the beloved mother of Humáyún and of his three sisters, 'Rose-blush,' 'Rosy-face,' and 'Rose-form': 'it was Sunday at midnight when I met Maham'—he had not seen her for very long[1]. One of his first visits was to his aunts. He had brought ninety-six of his women relations from Kábul, and he

[1] Maham Begum was of the family of Sultán Husain of Herát. Among Bábar's other wives we have already heard of his cousin 'Áïsha, the daughter of Sultán Ahmad, who was betrothed to him at the age of five, married whilst he was in difficulties at Khojend, and deserted him before the Uzbeg conquest of Táshkend. Her child lived only a few days. Her youngest sister, Ma'súma, fell in love with Bábar at Herát, and married him at Kábul, where she died in giving birth to a daughter, whom he named Ma'súma after her, and who married her cousin Muhammad Zamán Mirza, grandson of Sultán Husain of Herát, and a capable general in Bábar's campaigns. Other wives were Zainab, daughter of Sultán Mahmúd of Hisár, whom he married when he captured Kábul; Dildár Agácha, mother of Hindál; Räïka; and a daughter of the Yúsufzái chief.

made a point of going to pay his respects to them every Friday when at Agra. When his wife remonstrated with him on his going out in the heat to see them, he replied that his aunts had neither father nor brother, and there was none but he to comfort them [1]. If no very devoted lover, Bábar was certainly an admirable 'family man.'

In the intervals of his campaigns he wrote that valuable description of Hindústán which displays his undiminished interest in natural history, and his singular quickness of observation and accurate commemoration of statistical details. Though he had conquered his new empire, he did not love it. 'The country and towns of Hindústán,' he writes, 'are extremely ugly. All its towns and lands have a uniform look; its gardens have no walls; the greater part of it is a level plain.' He found 'the plains' monotonous after the mountain scenery of Kábul and the well-watered orchards of Farghána.

> 'Hindústán,' he adds, 'is a country that has few pleasures to recommend it. The people are not handsome. They have no idea of the charms of friendly society. They have no genius, no intellectual comprehension, no politeness, no kindness or fellow-feeling, no ingenuity or mechanical invention in planning or executing their handicrafts, no skill or knowledge in design or architecture. They have no good horses, no good flesh, no grapes or musk-melons [2], no good fruits, no

[1] The story is told in Gul-badan's *Memoirs*, and by Mr. H. Beveridge.

[2] India, it is said, owes both these fruits to Bábar's horticulture. Before he died he enjoyed grapes and musk-melons of his own growing.

ice or cold water, no good food or bread in their bazars, no baths or colleges, or candles or torches—never a candlestick!'

He might have modified this sweeping condemnation if he had lived longer in India and seen more of its races, and indeed he does admit that there are advantages even in India,—for example, in the abundance of workmen of all trades, and that 'the climate during the rains is very pleasant'; but on the whole 'the chief excellency of Hindústán is that it is a big country, with plenty of gold and silver.' But his perverse prejudice was deeply rooted, and one can see that even from the throne at Agra he looks back with regret to his own land, the land of melons and cool waters. Writing in February, 1529, to his old general, Khwája Kalán, in Afghánistán, in the midst of his triumphs, he says:—

'The affairs of Hindústán have at length been brought to some degree of order, and I trust in Almighty God that the time is near at hand when, through His favour, everything will be quite settled here. As soon as that is done I shall set out for your quarters, God willing, without losing a moment. How can the delights of those lands ever be erased from the heart? How can one like me, who has vowed abstinence and purity of life, possibly forget the delicious melons and grapes of that happy land? The other day they brought me a musk-melon: as I cut it up I felt a deep home-sickness, and sense of exile from my native land, and I could not help weeping.'

He has forgotten nothing of the beauties of his own Farghána, or of Kábul, the country of his adoption.

He orders repairs of the castle and great mosque, as if he were on the spot. There is a portico that must be seen to, and a garden that needs more water, a plantation that should be renewed, and orchards to be sown with 'beautiful and sweet-smelling flowers and shrubs.' He remembers with regret the joyous days he spent by the Kábul river, yet he is glad that he has had strength to reform. He admits that he 'had much difficulty in reconciling himself to the desert of penitence,' but he persevered:—

> Distraught I am since that I gave up wine;
> Confused, to nothing doth my soul incline.
> Regret did once my penitence beget;
> Now penitence induces worse regret.

'Excuse me,' he continues, 'for wandering into these follies. For God's sake, do not think amiss of me for them. I wrote last year the quatrain I quoted, and indeed last year my desire and longing for wine and conviviality were excessive beyond measure; so much that I have even found myself shedding tears of vexation and disappointment. This year, thank God, these troubles are over, and this I ascribe chiefly to my occupying my mind with poetry. Let me advise you too to adopt a life of abstinence.'

Writing a little earlier (Nov. 13, 1528) to his eldest son, Humáyún, to congratulate him on the birth of his first child, he is full of interest in the political state of the Oxus country. Matters had arrived there at a point in which it seemed possible that the throne of Samarkand might be recovered; and Bábar enjoins his son to advance with the support of his brothers to 'Hisár, Samarkand, or Merv, as may be most advisable. . . . This is the time for you to court danger and hardship, and show your valour in arms. Fail not to quit yourself strenuously to meet every emergency: indolence and ease agree ill with kingship.' If the attack succeed, Bábar will make an imperial government of Samarkand, with Humáyún on the throne.

The letter is full of good advice, not only as to the campaign (which never came off), but on various matters of conduct; Humáyún is to act handsomely by his brother Kamrán, the ruler of Kábul; he is not to complain of his own loneliness in Badakhshán—it is unworthy of a prince;—he is to consult his Begs and ministers, avoid private parties, and call all the court to public levees twice every day; and pay special deference to Khwája Kalán, and keep up the strength and discipline of the army. Small faults do not escape the parental critic. 'You have indeed written me letters,' says Bábar, 'but you certainly never read them over: had you attempted to read them you would have found it impossible.' Bábar himself could hardly make them out, with their crabbed writing—addressed to the man who invented the special script called the Bábari hand!—and their misspellings, and attempts at far-fetched idioms. 'Write unaffectedly,' says the critic, 'clearly, with plain words, which saves trouble to both writer and reader.' 'The language of kings,' it was said, 'is the king of languages,' and Bábar well understood how to write the royal tongue.

Not long after this, when the hopes of a re-conquest of Samarkand were over, Humáyún felt a longing to be with his father again[1], and set off from Badakhshán with impetuous haste, giving no notice of his coming. He found his parents at Agra:—

'I was just talking with his mother about him when in he came. His presence opened our hearts like rosebuds, and made our eyes shine like torches. It was my rule to keep open table every day, but on this occasion I gave feasts in his honour, and showed him every kind of distinction. We lived together for some time in the greatest intimacy. The truth is that his conversation had an inexpressible charm, and he realized absolutely the ideal of perfect manhood.'

How devotedly Bábar loved his son was seen a few months later, when the young man was brought back by boat from his country estate at Sambhal in the last stage of fever. The doctors were powerless, and it was suggested that nothing could save him but some supreme sacrifice to God. Bábar eagerly caught at the hope, and resolved at once to lay down his life for

[1] The following account is from a most interesting fragment appended to Bábar's Memoirs, which does not occur in the Persian or Turki texts of the complete work (Pavet de Courteille, ii. 457-460). Dr. Teufel (*Zeitschr. D.M.G.*, xxxvii, 141 ff.) endeavours to show that part of this fragment is translated from Abu-l-Fazl's *Akbar-náma*. and therefore a forgery; but it is quite possible that Abú-l-Fazl. as Mr. Beveridge suggests, may have heard the story from Bábar's daughter Gul-badan, or from Shaikh Zain-ad-dín. There are, however, linguistic difficulties and other differences from the general style of the Memoirs which are not easily reconciled.

his son. In vain the wise men remonstrated, and begged him to give riches and treasure, or the great diamond of the Rájas—anything but himself. 'Is there any stone,' he answered, 'that can be weighed against my son? Rather shall I pay his ransom myself, for he is in a grievous case, and my strength must bear his weakness.' He entered his son's chamber, and going to the head of the bed, walked gravely three times round the sick man, saying the while: 'On me be all that thou art suffering.' One thinks of the great scene in *Alcestis*:—

> σὺ τὸν αὑτᾶς
> ἔτλας πόσιν ἀντὶ σᾶς ἀμεῖψαι
> ψυχᾶς ἐξ Ἅιδα. κούφα σοι
> χθὼν ἐπάνωθε πέσοι.

'I have prevailed,' at last he was heard to cry; 'I have taken it!' Indeed, in his own words: 'At that moment I felt myself quite borne down, whilst he became buoyant and well. He arose in complete health, and I—I sank down in extreme illness. I called the chief men of the empire and the persons of greatest influence, and putting their hands in Humáyún's in token of investiture, I solemnly proclaimed him my successor, and assigned him the throne.'

These were probably almost the last words Bábar wrote,—if, indeed, he wrote them at all. The frequent illnesses from which he had suffered in India, culminating in the nervous prostration that succeeded his anxiety for his son, had undermined his great strength. On December 26, 1530, he passed away in his beautiful garden-palace at Agra—a man of only forty-eight, a king of thirty-six years—but years crowded with events, with hardships, tumult, and strenuous energy. The boy prince who had fought for his heritage long and indomitably with hordes of savage Mongols and Uzbegs, and only relinquished the hope of his ancestral throne after a struggle of twenty years, had at last found the way to a greater and nobler empire—whose splendour and ancient glory he had not yet learned to realize—but which he left, a magnificent heirloom, for his grandson Akbar to cherish and enrich.

Bábar lies in his grave in the garden on the hill at Kábul, which he had chosen for his tomb,—'the sweetest spot of the neighbourhood,'—surrounded by those he loved, by the sweet-smelling flowers of his choice, and the cool running stream, beside which he once delighted to sit and gaze on the beautiful world. The people still flock to the spot, and offer prayers at the simple mosque which an august descendant built in memory of the founder of the Indian Empire. Bábar was dead, but he had done what nothing could efface.

> Death makes no conquest of this Conqueror,
> For now he lives in Fame.

INDEX

THE END.

WORKS BY STANLEY LANE-POOLE.

Life of Edward William Lane 8vo, pp. 138. Williams & Norgate. 1877.

The People of Turkey. Edited. Two vols. 8vo, pp. xxxi, 281; x, 352. Murray. 1878.

Lane's Selections from the Kuran. Edited. 8vo, pp. cxii, 173. Trübner. 1879.

Egypt. Fcap. 8vo, pp. xii, 200. Sampson Low. 1881.

The Speeches and Table-Talk of the Prophet Mohammad. 18mo, pp. lxiii, 196. Macmillan's 'Golden Treasury' Series. 1882; re-issue, 1893.

Le Koran, sa Poésie et ses Lois. 24mo, pp. vi, 112. Leroux. 1882.

Studies in a Mosque. 1883. Second Edition. 8vo, pp. viii, 326. Eden. 1893.

Arabian Society in the Middle Ages. Edited. 8vo, pp. xvi, 283. Chatto. 1883.

Picturesque Palestine, Sinai, and Egypt. Egypt. 4to, pp. 121–234. Virtue. 1883.

Social Life in Egypt. 4to, pp. vi, 138. Virtue. 1883.

Prose Writings of Jonathan Swift. 8vo, pp. xxx, 284. Paul. 1884.

Notes for a Bibliography of Swift. 8vo, pp. 36. Elliot Stock. 1884.

Letters and Journals of Jonathan Swift. 8vo, pp. xv, 292. Paul. 1885.

The Life of General F. R. Chesney, R.A. Edited. 8vo, pp. xxiii, 279. Allen. 1885.

The Art of the Saracens in Egypt. 8vo, pp. xviii, 264. Chapman. 1886.

The Moors in Spain. 8vo, pp. xx, 285. Unwin. 1887.

Turkey. 8vo, pp. xix, 373. Unwin. 1888.

The Life of the Rt. Hon. Stratford Canning, Viscount Stratford de Redcliffe, K.G. 2 vols. 8vo, pp. xxix, 519; xviii, 475. Longmans. 1888.
Popular Edition. pp. xx, 377. Longmans. 1890.

Thirty Years of Colonial Government. From the Papers of the Rt. Hon. Sir G. F. Bowen, G.C.M.G. 2 vols. pp. viii, 460; viii, 467. Longmans. 1889.

The Barbary Corsairs. 8vo, pp. xviii, 316. Unwin. 1890.

Sir Richard Church, C.B., G.C.H. 8vo, pp. iv, 73. Longmans. 1890.

Stories from the Arabian Nights. 3 vols. 16mo, pp. vii, 338, 331, 346. Putnam. 1891.

The History of the Moghul Emperors illustrated by their Coins. pp. clxxvii. Constable. 1892.

Cairo: Sketches of its History, Monuments, and Social Life. 8vo, pp. xiv, 320. Virtue. 1892. Third Edition, 1898.

Works by Stanley Lane-Poole.

Aurangzib. 'Rulers of India' Series. 8vo, pp. 212. Clarendon Press. 1893.

Lane's Arabic-English Lexicon. Edited. Vols. 6–8. Imp. 4to, pp. xxxix, 2221–3064. Williams & Norgate. 1877–1893.

The Life of Sir Harry Parkes, H. M. Minister to China and Japan. 2 vols. 8vo, pp. xxvi, 512; xxi, 477. Macmillan. 1894.

Cairo Fifty Years Ago. By E. W. LANE. Edited. 8vo, pp. xvi, 162. Murray. 1896.

Catalogue of the Museum of Arab Art at Cairo. By HERZ BEY. Edited. 8vo pp. xviii, 91. Quaritch. 1896.

The Life of Saladin. 8vo, pp. xiii, 416. Putnam. 1898.

NUMISMATIC WORKS.

Catalogue of the Collection of Oriental Coins belonging to Colonel C. Seton Guthrie, R.E. Fasc. I. pp. viii, 38. Austin. 1874.

International Numismata Orientalia. Part II.—Coins of the Turkumans. 4to, pp. xii, 44. Trübner. 1875.

Essays in Oriental Numismatics. Three Series. 3 vols. 8vo, 1874, 1877, 1892.

Catalogue of Oriental Coins in the British Museum. Printed by order of the Trustees. 10 vols. 8vo. (Ouvrage couronné par l'Institut de France, 1881.)

Vol. I. THE KHALIFS. pp. xx, 263. 1875.
II. MOHAMMADAN DYNASTIES. pp. xii, 279. 1876.
III. THE TURKUMANS. pp. xxvi, 305. 1877.
IV. EGYPT. pp. xxx, 279. 1879.
V. THE MOORS AND ARABIA. pp. lii, 175. 1880.
VI. THE MONGOLS. pp. lxxv, 300. 1881.
VII. BUKHARA. pp. xlviii, 131. 1882.
VIII. THE TURKS. pp. li, 431. 1883.
IX, X. ADDITIONS: 1875–1889, and General Index. 2 vols. pp. 420, 460. 1889, 1890.

Catalogue of Indian Coins in the British Museum. 3 vols. 8vo.

Vol. I. SULTANS OF DEHLI. pp. xiv, 199. 1884.
II. MUHAMMADAN STATES. pp lxxx, 239. 1885.
III. MOGHUL EMPERORS. pp. cliii, 401. 1892.

Catalogue of Arabic Glass Weights in the British Museum. 8vo, pp. xxxv, 127. 1891.

Coins and Medals: their place in History and Art. By the Authors of the British Museum Official Catalogues. Edited. 8vo, pp. x, 286. Stock. 1885. Third Edition, 1894.

Catalogue of the Mohammadan Coins in the Bodleian Library, Oxford. pp. xvi, 55. Clarendon Press. 1888.

Catalogue of the Arabic Coins in the Khedivial Library at Cairo. 8vo pp. xv, 384. Quaritch.

RULERS OF INDIA

THE CLARENDON PRESS SERIES OF INDIAN HISTORICAL RETROSPECTS.

Edited by SIR W. W. HUNTER, K.C.S.I., M.A., LL.D.

The following 28 volumes have been already published:—

I. *A BRIEF HISTORY OF THE INDIAN PEOPLES*, by SIR WILLIAM WILSON HUNTER, K.C.S.I. Twenty-second Edition; Eighty-fourth thousand. Price 3s. 6d.

II. *BÁBAR: the Founder of the Mughal Dynasty.* By STANLEY LANE-POOLE, Esq., M.A., Professor of Arabic, Trinity College, Dublin; Author of *The Life of Lord Stratford de Redcliffe.* 2s. 6d.

III. *AKBAR: and the Rise of the Mughal Empire*, by COLONEL MALLESON, C.S.I., Author of *A History of the Indian Mutiny; The History of Afghanistan.* Fifth thousand. 2s. 6d.

IV. *ALBUQUERQUE: and the Early Portuguese Settlements in India*, by H. MORSE STEPHENS, Esq., M.A., Balliol College, formerly Lecturer on Indian History at Cambridge, Author of *The French Revolution; The Story of Portugal, &c.* Third thousand. 2s. 6d.

V. *AURANGZÍB: and the Decay of the Mughal Empire*, by STANLEY LANE-POOLE, Esq., M.A., Author of *The Coins of the Mughal Emperors; The Life of Stratford Canning; Catalogue of Indian Coins in the British Museum, &c.* Third Thousand. 2s. 6d.

VI. *MADHAVA RAO SINDHIA: and the Hindú Reconquest of India*, by H. G. KEENE, Esq., M.A., C.I.E., Author of *The Moghul Empire, &c.* Third Thousand. 2s. 6d.

VII. *LORD CLIVE: and the Establishment of the English in India*, by COLONEL MALLESON, C.S.I. Third Thousand. 2s. 6d.

VIII. *DUPLEIX: and the Struggle for India by the European Nations*, by COLONEL MALLESON, C.S.I., Author of *The History of the French in India, &c.* Fifth Thousand. 2s. 6d.

IX. ***WARREN HASTINGS:** and the Founding of the British Administration,* by CAPTAIN L. J. TROTTER, Author of *India under Victoria, &c.* Fifth thousand. 2*s.* 6*d.*

X. ***THE MARQUESS CORNWALLIS:** and the Consolidation of British Rule,* by W. S. SETON-KARR, Esq., sometime Foreign Secretary to the Government of India, Author of *Selections from the Calcutta Gazettes,* 3 vols. (1784–1805). Fourth thousand. 2*s.* 6*d.*

XI. ***HAIDAR ALÍ AND TIPÚ SULTÁN:** and the Struggle with the Muhammadan Powers of the South,* by LEWIN BENTHAM BOWRING, Esq., C.S.I., sometime Private Secretary to the Viceroy (Lord Canning) and Chief Commissioner of Mysore, Author of *Eastern Experiences.* Third thousand. 2*s.* 6*d.*

XII. ***THE MARQUESS WELLESLEY:** and the Development of the Company into the Supreme Power in India,* by the Rev. W. H. HUTTON, B.D., Fellow and Tutor of St. John's College, Oxford. Third thousand. 2*s.* 6*d.*

XIII. ***THE MARQUESS OF HASTINGS:** and the Final Overthrow of the Maráthá Power,* by MAJOR ROSS OF BLADENSBURG, C.B., Coldstream Guards; F.R.G.S. 2*s.* 6*d.*

XIV. ***MOUNTSTUART ELPHINSTONE:** and the Making of South-Western India,* by J. S. COTTON, Esq., M.A., formerly Fellow of Queen's College, Oxford, Author of *The Decennial Statement of the Moral and Material Progress and Condition of India,* presented to Parliament (1885), &c. Third thousand. 2*s.* 6*d.*

XV. ***SIR THOMAS MUNRO:** and the British Settlement of the Madras Presidency,* by JOHN BRADSHAW, Esq., M.A., LL.D., late Inspector of Schools, Madras. 2*s.* 6*d.*

XVI. ***EARL AMHERST:** and the British Advance eastwards to Burma,* chiefly from unpublished papers of the Amherst family, by Mrs. ANNE THACKERAY RITCHIE, Author of *Old Kensington, &c.*, and RICHARDSON EVANS, Esq. 2*s.* 6*d.*

XVII. *LORD WILLIAM BENTINCK: and the Company as a Governing and Non-trading Power*, by DEMETRIUS BOULGER, Esq., Author of *England and Russia in Central Asia; The History of China, &c.* Third thousand. 2s. 6d.

XVIII. *EARL OF AUCKLAND: and the First Afghan War*, by CAPTAIN L. J. TROTTER, Author of *India under Victoria, &c.* 2s. 6d.

XIX. *VISCOUNT HARDINGE: and the Advance of the British Dominions into the Punjab*, by his Son and Private Secretary, the Right Hon. VISCOUNT HARDINGE. Third thousand. 2s. 6d.

XX. *RANJIT SINGH: and the Sikh Barrier between our Growing Empire and Central Asia*, by SIR LEPEL GRIFFIN, K.C.S.I., Author of *The Punjab Chiefs, &c.* Fourth thousand. 2s. 6d.

XXI. *JOHN RUSSELL COLVIN: the last Lieutenant-Governor of the North-Western Provinces under the Company*, by his son, SIR AUCKLAND COLVIN, K.C.S.I., late Lieutenant-Governor of the North-Western Provinces. 2s. 6d.

XXII. *THE MARQUESS OF DALHOUSIE: and the Final Development of the Company's Rule*, by SIR WILLIAM WILSON HUNTER, K.C.S.I., M.A. Seventh thousand. 2s. 6d.

XXIII. *CLYDE AND STRATHNAIRN: and the Suppression of the Great Revolt*, by MAJOR-GENERAL SIR OWEN TUDOR BURNE, K.C.S.I., sometime Military Secretary to the Commander-in-Chief in India. Fourth thousand. 2s. 6d.

XXIV. *EARL CANNING: and the Transfer of India from the Company to the Crown*, by SIR HENRY S. CUNNINGHAM, K.C.I.E., M.A., Author of *British India and its Rulers, &c.* Fourth thousand. 2s. 6d.

XXV. *LORD LAWRENCE: and the Reconstruction of India under the Crown*, by SIR CHARLES UMPHERSTON AITCHISON, K.C.S.I., LL.D., formerly Foreign Secretary to the Government of India, and Lieutenant-Governor of the Punjab. Fourth thousand. 2s. 6d.

XXVI. *THE EARL OF MAYO: and the Consolidation of the Queen's Rule in India*, by SIR WILLIAM WILSON HUNTER, K.C.S.I., M.A., LL.D. Third thousand. *2s. 6d.*

SUPPLEMENTARY VOLUMES.

XXVII. *JAMES THOMASON: and the British Settlement of North-Western India*, by SIR RICHARD TEMPLE, Bart., M.P., formerly Lieutenant-Governor of Bengal, and Governor of Bombay Price 3s. *6d.*

XXVIII. *SIR HENRY LAWRENCE: The Pacificator.* By Lieut.-General J. J. McLEOD INNES, R.E., V.C. Price 3s. *6d.*